BEYOND THE DEATH PENALTY

The Development in Catholic Social Teaching

Edited by
JOE HOLLAND, PH.D.
Professor of Philosophy and Religion, Saint Thomas University of Miami
President, Pax Romana Catholic Movement for Intellectual and Cultural Affairs, Washington DC

and

D. MICHAEL MCCARRON, PH.D.
Executive Director
Florida Catholic Conference, Tallahassee, Florida

PAX ROMANA CENTER FOR
INTERNATIONAL STUDY OF CATHOLIC SOCIAL TEACHING

Saint Thomas University
16401 NW 37th Avenue, Miami, Florida 33054 USA
Phone: 1.305.474.6913 / Fax: 1.305.474.6915
Email: paxromana@stu.edu
Website: www.pax-romana-center-cst.org

ISBN: 1-4196-7310-6

Library of Congress Control Number: 2007905299

First Edition August 2007

This book has been developed from a project titled
"Catholic Social Teaching against the Death Penalty".
and has been jointly produced by

FLORIDA COUNCIL OF CATHOLIC SCHOLARSHIP
A scholarly society established in 1996
at the invitation of the Florida Catholic Conference

and

PAX ROMANA CENTER FOR
INTERNATIONAL STUDY OF CATHOLIC SOCIAL TEACHING
A division of
Pax Romana/Catholic Movement for Intellectual and Cultural Affairs USA

The offices of the Florida Council and the Pax Romana Center
are both hosted by and located at

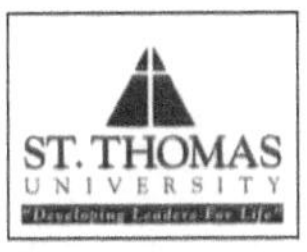

SAINT THOMAS UNIVERSITY
16401 NW 37th Avenue, Miami, Florida 33054 USA
Phone: 1.628.6546 / Website: www.stu.edu

In Memory of the late Rev. Jorge Sardiñas,
deceased Professor of Fine Arts
at Saint Thomas University,
with gratitude for the moving work of art used on the cover
and for the wonderful gift of his life of service.

"Blessed are they who show mercy;
mercy shall be theirs."

THE GOSPEL OF MATTHEW
Chapter 5, Verse

TABLE OF CONTENTS

APPENDICES

My Dear Brothers and Sisters in the Lord:

I congratulate the Florida Council of Catholic Scholarship and the Pax Romana Center for their production of this fine work, BEYOND THE DEATH PENALTY: THE DEVELOPMENT IN CATHOLIC SOCIAL TEACHING. *This work contains a thorough consideration of our Church teaching on the subject, which in sum is that only when society cannot be protected in any other way is the death penalty justified. As the Florida bishops have said, "Every human life must be respected, even lives of those that fail to show that respect for others. The sacredness of human life and the dignity of the human person remain, even for one who has violated the rights of others by taking human life."*

For more than 25 years, both the Florida and national bishops have been speaking out on the death penalty as it is administered in our country. Today, we are amidst a national Catholic campaign to end the use of the death penalty, to build a constituency for life, not death. As our late Holy Father, Pope John Paul II, reminded us during his trip to St. Louis, Missouri in January 1999: "The new evangelization calls for followers of Christ who are unconditionally pro-life: who will proclaim, celebrate and serve the Gospel of Life in every situation." May this work positively impact those who study it, reinforcing the belief in the unique dignity of every individual, and the sacredness of all human life.

Sincerely yours in the Lord,

+ John C. Favalora
Archbishop of Miami

Dear readers,

A Catholic university serves as a forum for dialogue about contemporary issues and as a bridge between the intellectual and artistic heritage of the Church and the lived-out experience of people. In this regard, our University is proud to have been a founding member of the Florida Council of Catholic Scholarship, and it is now honored to join with the Pax Romana Center for International Study of Catholic Social Teaching in the production of this text, BEYOND THE DEATH PENALTY: THE DEVELOPMENT IN CATHOLIC SOCIAL TEACHING.

St. Thomas University is rooted in the tradition of Catholic Social Teaching and supports its consistent ethic of life, as does this book. The chapters in the book will be most helpful in fostering discussion of the historical and political evaluation of capital punishment and in developing an appreciation for the Church's willingness over time to struggle with this issue.

This book is a fine example of the work being done in our Catholic universities by scholars engaged in teaching and research. Such work confirms our commitment to the challenge given by the late Pope John Paul II's apostolic constitution on Catholic universities, EX CORDE ECCLESIAE, *that "a Catholic university is a place of research, where scholars scrutinize reality with the methods proper to each academic discipline, and so contribute to the treasury of human knowledge."*

I am grateful to the editors, Joe Holland, Ph.D. and D. Michael McCarron, Ph.D., and to all those scholars who participated in this worthwhile project.

Sincerely yours,

Rev. Msgr. Franklyn M. Casale
President, Saint Thomas University, Miami Gardens, Florida

ACKNOWLEDGEMENTS

Profound thanks are due to the many authors whose essays appear in this volume. At the same time, they deserve great gratitude for their patience in waiting for several years for these essays to be published. Only recently were the resources of time and money found to make this publishing possible.

Profound thanks are also due to the many people who proof-read this book, especially to Dr. Nancy Powers, formerly with the Florida Catholic Conference. Extra special thanks go to César J. Baldelomar, Research Coordinator for the Pax Romana Center for International Study of Catholic Social Teaching. Without his countless hours of labor, the book still would not have seen the light of day.

Profound thanks also go to Msgr. Franklyn M. Casale, President of Saint Thomas University in Miami Gardens, Florida. He convened the first meeting of the Florida Council of Catholic Scholarship, and he has been extremely supportive of both the Florida Council and the Pax Romana Center, with both hosted by Saint Thomas.

In addition, deep gratitude is owed to all the Catholic bishops of Florida, first for their leadership in defense of human life, including on behalf of the Catholic campaign against the death penalty. They were most encouraging for the formation of the Florida Council, and later in supporting it over the years. In particular, deep gratitude is due to Archbishop John Clement Favalora for his leadership in the Archdiocese of Miami on behalf of human life, and for his encouragement for all the work of Saint Thomas University, which is sponsored by the Archdiocese. Special gratitude is also due to Bishop Felipe Estévez, Auxiliary Bishop of the Archdiocese of Miami for his supportive role as Episcopal Adviser to the Pax Romana Center.

1

INTRODUCING THE QUESTION

JOE HOLLAND, PH.D.

Professor of Philosophy & Religion,
Saint Thomas University, Miami Gardens, Florida
President, Pax Romana
Catholic Movement for Intellectual & Cultural Affairs USA
Washington DC

This Introduction has been developed from a White Paper prepared by the author and originally issued on 10 April 2000 in conjunction with the state-wide Florida Symposium on the Death Penalty, organized by the Florida Council of Catholic Scholarship and held at St. Vincent de Paul Regional Seminary in Boynton Beach, Florida.

We of the Florida Council of Catholic Scholarship together with Pax Romana Center for the International Study of Catholic Social Teaching (with both located at Saint Thomas University in Miami Gardens, Florida) invite all disciples of Jesus in the Catholic churches and other Christian churches of Florida and elsewhere, all people of other religious traditions, and all people of good will, to study the hotly debated question of the death penalty. We speak especially to Catholics in Florida, for we are told that grass-roots support for the death penalty is substantial among Catholics here. Yet research has shown that, when ordinary people carefully reflect on this issue, they tend to favor its abolition.

To help grass-roots Catholics with this examination, we have prepared a well-researched yet easy-reading study-book on the contemporary Catholic challenge to the death penalty. This book acknowledges that in times past official Catholic teachers, namely the popes and the bishops, often supported the death penalty as a means of community self-defense against internal violent aggressors. In recent times, however, as the book demonstrates, the popes and the Catholic bishops of the world have begun to teach that in practically all cases the traditional justification for death penalty no longer applies. As a result, recently the popes and the bishops have been conducting a worldwide campaign against the death penalty.

In addition, most recently the late Pope John Paul II asked forgiveness from the people of the world for the many times in past ages when leaders in the Catholic Church themselves used the death penalty as a weapon against "heretics" and "unbelievers." He clearly stated that this was sinful. Unfortunately this sad legacy may have contributed to current support for the death penalty.

The reasons for the current Catholic campaign against the death penalty are multiple and profound.

- There are now truly humane means to protect the community against murderous criminals (namely life in prison without parole), so that the community itself does not need to violently kill yet another human being.
- Human life is given by God as sacred, and its sacredness does not depend on our good or evil behavior.
- The "consistent ethic of life" requires that, in opposing abortion and euthanasia, we also oppose the death penalty.
- There is no "humane" form of the death penalty, and every form of execution – be it by beheading, the guillotine, hanging, a firing squad, the electric chair, poison gas, or a lethal injection – is the brutal and violent killing of a sacred human life.

- We are now discovering, due especially to DNA testing, that many death row inmates have been wrongly convicted and are actually innocent of the murders for which they were sentenced to death. Reportedly Florida has led the nation in this problem.
- There appears to be great racial prejudice in the application of the death penalty, especially in the United States where, for example, blacks convicted of murdering whites are executed at disproportionate rates.
- Those who have been executed for the death penalty include a range of different persons who are not responsible for their actions and who should be removed from the community, but who should not be put to death: for example, the mentally retarded and the criminally insane.
- The death penalty has been shown by repeated research not to serve as a deterrent to violent crime.
- The death penalty does not bring the "closure" of true peace and healing to victims of crime, nor to their families. As we know in the Christian tradition, true peace and healing comes only with forgiveness – however understandably difficult that may be.
- The death penalty advances a brutalizing celebration of violence that is rapidly spreading across our media, our families, and our communities, and worst of all is now infecting many of our youth.
- The death penalty fails to accept the Christian teaching that even the worst sinners may one day seek forgiveness and be spiritually saved.
- Across the world, most countries have in principle or in practice eliminated the death penalty.

The present pro-death penalty policies of the United States, and especially those of Florida, stand as among the most brutal and uncivilized in the entire world. With great tragedy, our nation and our state have sought the simplistic and erroneous solution of capital punishment.

Recently the popes and the bishops have proposed that this is part of a wider and growing modern "Culture of Death." This Culture of Death undermines the sacred dignity of the human person by finding ever-new excuses to commit violent acts of killing. In the modern Culture of Death, we see an expanding turn to violent and deadly solutions proposed for the "social problems" not only of dangerous criminals, but also of so-called "unwanted" children alive in the womb, and even of so-called "useless" elderly and handicapped persons.

Jesus, who himself was violently executed by officials of the government of the Roman Empire, told us that violent killing is not the way to justice or to peace. Today our bishops are again reaffirming Jesus' teaching, and the late Pope John Paul II has even called Jesus' teaching a "Gospel of Life." They are proclaiming the sacredness of life, and speaking out against all violent killing. They are defending the unborn, the elderly, the handicapped, the poor, those in prison, and even those condemned to death.

In the 25th Chapter of the Gospel of Matthew, Jesus tells us how we will be judged at the end of the world. One of his criteria for judgment is how we respond to those in prisons and to all the least of our brothers and sisters. To the ones who visited those in prison and who cared for the least, Jesus promises eternal life (verses 44-46). Perhaps the debate over the death penalty is not simply about crime and punishment, but also about our salvation.

2

ENGAGING THE PUBLIC DEBATE

D. MICHAEL MCCARRON, PH.D.
Executive Director
Florida Catholic Conference, Tallahassee, Florida

WORKING TOWARD CONSENSUS AGAINST THE DEATH PENALTY

In recent years, Americans, and particularly Catholics, have been engaged in reexamination of their thoughts and feelings about the death penalty.

This introspection was spurred especially by the late Pope John Paul II's visit to St. Louis in January 1999, where he addressed Catholics and Americans in general in his call for a consensus to end the death penalty. At the Papal Mass in St Louis, Missouri on January 27, 1999, the pope said:

> *The new evangelization calls for followers of Christ who are unconditionally pro-life: who will proclaim, celebrate and serve the Gospel of Life in every situation. A sign of hope is the increasing recognition that the dignity of human life must never be taken away, even in the case of someone who has done great evil. Modern society has the means of protecting itself, without definitively denying criminals a chance to reform (cf. Evangelium Vitae, 27). I renew the appeal I made most recently at Christmas for a consensus to end the death penalty, which is both cruel and unnecessary.*

This message, reflected in the headlines of major newspapers across the country, was only bolstered by the late Holy Father's successful appeal to Missouri Governor Mel Carnahan for the commutation of sentence of death row inmate Darrell Mease. The late Holy Father's actions, a clear example of engaging the public debate, were soon to be followed by other Church leaders taking advantage of their right and responsibility to inform the public debate on the death penalty.

Early in the new millennium, Florida's Catholic bishops communicated their opposition to the death penalty to every member of the Florida House and Senate, as they began a January Special Legislative Session on the death penalty called by Governor Jeb Bush. Also in January, Cardinal Francis George of Chicago, speaking before the Illinois Legislature on behalf of the Catholic Conference of Illinois, urged a moratorium on the death penalty in that state. Soon after, Governor George Ryan declared a moratorium.[1]

In early February of that year, then president of the National Conference of Catholic Bishops, Bishop Joseph A. Fiorenza of Galveston-Houston, wrote to President Clinton asking that he suspend federal executions. The following week, the Texas bishops wrote to Governor George W. Bush urging that he withhold executions in a state that has accounted for more than one-third of all U.S. executions since 1976.[2] On February 22, Cardinal Anthony J. Bevalacqua of Philadelphia testified before the Pennsylvania Senate urging that state to adopt a two-year moratorium on executions.

While these bishops were engaging the public debate, growing numbers of Americans were pondering what Pope John Paul II called "increasingly mature forms of respect for life and for the dignity of every person." The United States is virtually alone in the Western world in preserving the death penalty as punishment. We are left in

---

1 Florida Catholic Conference Archives, State Catholic Conference Files, see Catholic Conferences of Illinois, Texas, and Pennsylvania.

2 Ibid. Also see *Our Sunday Visitor*, March 12, 2000.

the company of Iran, Iraq, Saudi Arabia, and China – countries from whom we have been known to distance ourselves in other instances because of their stance on human rights violations.

American Bishops Begin Engagement in Death Penalty Debate

Involvement by the Catholic Church in America in the death penalty debate is not a recent phenomenon. Opposition to the injustices inherent in capital punishment can be traced back more than a quarter-century.

The United States Supreme Court struck down the death penalty in the 1972 landmark case of *Furman v. Georgia.* This five-four decision found existing state laws on capital punishment to be a violation of the Eighth Amendment, cruel and unusual punishment, and administered in an arbitrary and capricious manner.[3] In 1976, the United States Supreme Court upheld newly adopted capital punishment statutes. To the dismay of Florida's bishops, theirs was the first state to re-instate the death penalty after this ruling.

Dr. James J. Megivern, Th.D.., Professor of Philosophy and Religion at University of North Carolina-Wilmington, made poignant observations about these events. He pointed to a "Bicentennial Bifurcation" that occurred on July 2, 1976, two days before our nation's 200th birthday, the day on which the U.S. Supreme Court reinstated capital punishment in its ruling of *Gregg v. Georgia.* The U.S. bishops near this same time began going in the opposite direction by expanding the consistent ethic of life philosophy to include defense of those charged with the death penalty.[4] In the ensuing years, this split between Church and State on this vital issue has only intensified. Today, Catholic and other church leaders are actively engaged in every

---

3 *Furman v. Georgia*, 408 U.S. 238, 92 S. CT. 2726 (1972).

4 James J. Megivern, "The Dilemma of Capital Punishment," United States Catholic Conference, Washington, D.C., 1995.

state where public policy proposals on the death penalty are under consideration.[5]

The Catholic Church has always taught that the state has the right and authority to impose capital punishment, but it has increasingly held that it ought not to make use of this right. A consistent message calling for remediation and mercy can be traced from the earliest Church teachings to the present-day opposition expressed by bishops in America and elsewhere. [6]

The Florida bishops, in their July 1990 statement against the death penalty entitled "Protection, Punishment, But Not Death," said:

> *In history, the Catholic Church has approved the death penalty. However, in 1976, in a carefully detailed statement, the Papal Commission on Justice and Peace expressed opposition to the death penalty. Pope John Paul II has frequently asked for clemency for persons condemned to death. In 1974, 1978, 1980, and 1984, the National Conference of Catholic Bishops issued statements opposing the death penalty. In 1976, the Bishops of Canada issued a statement opposing the death penalty. In the past 25 years, a number of state conferences of Bishops and a number of individual Bishops have written against the death penalty.*[7]

---

5 See *Catholics Against Capital Punishment*, "Bibliography of Statements by U.S. Catholic Bishops on the Death Penalty: 1972-1997," August 8, 1997.

6 Tertullian (early Christian theologian) and Lactantius (early Christian apologist) held in the third century that "there could be no exception to God's law against taking human life." Pope Leo I (fifth century) and Nicholas I (ninth century) insisted that the Church itself shun the use of the sword. The Council of Toledo (675) and the Fourth Lateran Council (1215) forbade clerics to take any part in the juridical process or sentence on a capital charge. See *New Catholic Encyclopedia*, 1967, Volume III, p. 80.

7 Catholic Bishops of Florida, Pastoral Statement, "Protection, Punishment, But Not Death," Statements of the Catholic Bishops of Florida, July 1990: pp. 145-146.

Responsibility of the Laity in Engaging Debate

Speaking on their own authority and through their state Catholic conferences, the bishops have exercised their right as citizens and their responsibility as religious teachers to shed light on the moral dimensions of public life, including the death penalty. But, as the bishops have consistently pointed out, it is not the responsibility of the bishops as teachers alone. The laity are also called "to be a community of conscience within the larger society" and to be meaningfully involved in public forums where faith and morals can play a constructive role.[8]

Every four years since the mid-1970s, the Administrative Board of the United States Catholic Conference (now the United States Conference of Catholic Bishops) has adopted a statement on political responsibility calling Catholics to active involvement in political life. While pointing out the Church's role to call attention to the moral and religious dimension of secular issues, the bishops have pointed to the need for individual Catholics to become informed, active, and responsible participants in the political process. "Participation in the process of governing is part of our democratic system. This communication to a legislator of a strongly held position on an issue of public policy thus fulfills both spiritual and civic purposes." [9]

Speaking in *Faithful Citizenship: Civic Responsibility for a New Millennium*, and specifically on the death penalty, the bishops said:

> *Society has a right and duty to defend itself against violent crime, and a duty to reach out to victims of crime. Yet, our nation's increasing re-*

---

8 *Faithful Citizenship: Civic Responsibility for a New Millennium*, A Statement of Political Responsibility by the Administrative Board of the U.S. Catholic Bishops, November 1999, p. 8.

9 *Proclaiming the Gospel of Life, Protecting the Least among Us, and Pursuing the Common Good*, Reflections on the 1996 Elections, United States Catholic Conference, September 1995.

liance on the death penalty is extremely troubling. Respect for human life must even include respect for those who have taken the lives of others. It has become clear, as Pope John Paul II has taught, that inflicting the penalty of death is cruel and unnecessary. The antidote to violence is not more violence. As part of our pro-life commitment, we encourage solutions to violent crime that reflect the dignity of the human person, urging our nation to abandon the use of capital punishment. Respect for human life and dignity is the necessary first step in building a civilization of life and love.

Clearly the bishops are important leaders in engaging the public debate; just as clear, the layperson has a role in engaging policymakers on this and other crucial questions involving life. And, while the Church does not become involved in partisan politics or electoral activity, this is appropriately the domain of the laity. The faithful have demonstrated growing appreciation for these responsibilities in recent years, assisted in this by state Catholic conferences, which have facilitated involvement through networks and legislative gatherings. Faithful citizens are increasingly advocating defense of parents' rights, the unborn, the frail elderly, the disabled and other instances where human life or human dignity have been coming under legal attack. It is only recently, however, that we see a new advocacy for truly "the least among us," the death row inmate. Encouragement by the Holy Father for the faithful to engage in this debate is slowly beginning to bear fruit.

Church Brings Consistent Teaching to Debate

Despite more than two decades of engagement by the Church in the debate surrounding capital punishment, it has been chiefly a back-burner concern for most of the faithful. At least in part this has been because of the very clear teaching regarding direct attacks on innocent human life, either through abortion or euthanasia. Today, however, more are beginning to appreciate that "our witness to respect for life shines most brightly when we demand respect for each and every human life, including the lives of those who fail to show that respect for others."[10]

Some advance the notion that capital punishment exists on the same moral plane as abortion. Abortion is the destruction of innocent human life. Capital punishment involves the execution of convicted killers. It is not moral equivalency that is urged here. Cardinal Bevalacqua of Philadelphia put it clearly: "The sacredness of human life and the dignity of the human person are not privileges we earn by good deeds, nor can they be forfeited for whatever crimes one commits."[11]

This teaching is not always an easy one for Catholics who have long understood the Church to teach that capital punishment is acceptable in cases of extreme gravity. There is, though, increasing acceptance of the teaching of John Paul II in his encyclical *The Gospel of Life*, also now reflected in the revised Catechism of the Catholic Church, that

> *. . . the nature and extent of the punishment must be carefully evaluated and decided upon, and ought not go to the extreme of executing the offender except in cases of absolute necessity: in other words, when it would not be possible to otherwise defend society. Today, however, as a result in the steady improvements in the organization of the penal system, such cases are very rare, if practically non-existent.* [12]

Still, what of Thomas Aquinas and Augustine? Everyone knows that they upheld the use of the death penalty. True enough, they did, but an examination of the foundation of their belief shows the consis-

---

10 United States Catholic Conference, *Living the Gospel of Life: A Challenge to American Catholics* (Washington, D.C.: United States Catholic Conference, 1998), No. 22.

11 Testimony by Anthony Cardinal Bevalacqua on 22 February 2000 to the Pennsylvania State Judiciary Committee.

12 Pope John Paul II, Encyclical, *The Gospel of Life*, 1995, No. 56. See also *The Catechism of the Catholic Church*, No. 2265-2667 (Revised 1998).

tency of Church teaching from its very beginning to the present day.[13] Both spoke against the use of the death penalty as a form of retribution and vengeance; both stressed the need for remediation in such penalties; both, along with other prominent and respected apologists before and after them, saw capital punishment as justified only as a means of protecting the whole body of society. It was their desire that justice be satisfied without taking life, and it may be said that their positions are reflected in Chapter 33, verse 11 of the Book of Ezekiel: "As I live says the Lord God, I swear I take no pleasure in the death of the wicked man, but rather in the wicked man's conversion, that he may live."

So, while some are suggesting that the Catholic Church's teaching on the death penalty has changed, it is perhaps more accurate to say that the traditional justification of capital punishment does not currently apply.[14] Our means of defending ourselves from violent assault no

---

13 St. Augustine in the fifth century, commenting on Romans 13:4, defended severity for the state of the social order, but praised the Christian instinct to temper such juridical sternness: "We do not wish to have the sufferings of the servants of God avenged by the infliction of precisely similar energies in the way of retaliation . . . but our desire is rather that justice be satisfied without the taking of their lives or the maiming of their bodies in any part . . . and that they be drawn away from their insane frenzy to the quietness of men in their sound judgment, or compelled to give up mischievous violence and betake themselves to some useful labor." (See St. Augustine, *Epistle 133,* No. 1.)

St. Thomas Aquinas made his classic defense of the death penalty on the grounds that "if a man be dangerous and infectious to the community, on account of some sin, it is praiseworthy and advantageous that he be killed in order to safeguard the common good." However, he proposed as a working jurisprudential norm that "in this life, penalties should rather be remedial than retributive." (See *Summa Theologiae* 2a2ae)

14 There were many other Old Testament scriptures that prescribed the death penalty for a wide variety of offenses. They included adultery (Leviticus 20:10); idolatry (Exodus 20:3); false prophecy in the name of God (Deuteronomy 18:20); laboring on the Sabbath (Exodus 31:14); striking or cursing or rebelling against a parent (Leviticus 19:3); and disobedience of religious authority (Deuteronomy 17:8). We must, however, look to the entire witness of the

longer require that we kill the offenders.[15] There may remain some universal situations where the death penalty would be justified as an act of defense; however, these are cases that, in the words of the Holy Father, "are very rare, if practically non-existent."[16] This is especially true in the Western World.

Protection, Punishment, But Not Death

The growing calls to end the death penalty – or at least to place a federal or state moratorium on executions – are based on several factors. Among these is the sense that it does not deter crimes, that it

---

Scriptures. Using the commandment "Thou shalt not kill" as our foundation (Exodus), let us examine some others that speak to this question. "As I live, says the Lord God, I swear I take no pleasure in the death of the wicked man, but rather in the wicked man's conversion, that he may live." (Ezekiel 33:11); "I set before you life and death; choose life." (Deuteronomy 30:19); "God, who is always merciful even when He punishes, put a mark on Cain, lest any who came upon him should kill him." (Genesis 4:15). And in the New Testament, "For any of you who have not sinned, let him cast the first stone." (John 8:7); "You have heard that it was said, "An eye for an eye, a tooth for a tooth," but I say to you not to resist the evildoers; on the contrary, if someone strikes you on the right cheek, turn to him the other also." (Matthew 5:38-39)

15 Many argue justification of the death penalty from the Scriptures, most often citing Old Testament verses such as "Whoever sheds the blood of man, by man shall his blood be shed." (Genesis 9:6); "When a man kills another after maliciously scheming to do so, you must take him even from my altar and put him to death." (Exodus 21:14); and especially, "if injury ensues, you shall give life for life, eye for eye, tooth for tooth, hand for hand." (Exodus 21:23-24). This latter seemingly harsh law was in actuality a radical call for moderation in the ancient Middle East. Prior to Mosaic Law, people in the Middle East did not limit retribution to "a life for a life." If someone was murdered, the family of the victim might lead an armed band, kill and torture the perpetrator, pillage the murderer's village, and rape or murder his relatives. Moses presented a radical new idea, a commandment from God insisting that the harshness of the punishment not exceed the ferocity of the crime.

16 Evangelium Vitae, No. 56.

discriminates against the poor and minorities, that innocent people can be and are executed, and that it is morally wrong.

The Florida bishops issued their first statement in opposition to the death penalty in 1972. Others followed it in 1979, 1983, 1984, 1990, and 1994. As of summer 2002, there are approximately 365 persons on death row in Florida, and as of summer 2003 some 56 executions have taken place since the death penalty was reinstated in this state. The July 6, 1990 statement of the Florida bishops, "Protection, Punishment, But Not Death," delineated multiple reasons why the death penalty should not be considered an appropriate form of punishment for murder or other serious crimes:

1. The death penalty contributes to disrespect for human dignity and human life. It contributes to the atmosphere of violence.
2. It is not a deterrent to crime. Empirical studies indicate that it has no effect as a deterrent: there is certainly no clear evidence that it is a deterrent. As the death penalty continues to be imposed in Florida, violence continues to escalate.
3. In its application it is discriminatory. The death penalty falls most often on the underprivileged – the indigent, the friendless, minorities, and ethnic groups.
4. Mistakes can be and have been made through which innocent persons die. This mistake is not remediable.
5. It precludes the possibility of reform or rehabilitation.
6. The legal imposition of the death penalty necessarily involves long delays, which in themselves become a form of cruel and unusual punishment.
7. The death penalty and its delays cause anguish to the family of the victim and to the family of the criminal.
8. The publicity attendant upon executions arouses animosity and escalates the level of violence.

9. There is no humane way for the state to kill someone. The electric chair, gas chamber, lethal injection, and the firing squad are all brutal in their application, and brutalize those who take part in them.

10. The ability of a judge to override a jury's recommendation of a life sentence is especially offensive.

It is a little known fact that Florida leads the nation in prisoners, twenty-five as of the date of this writing, who have been released after years on death row, when later the state admitted they were innocent or wrongly convicted. Death row may very well continue to include persons who are innocent; in certainty, it includes those persons who were sentenced to death by a judge who overrode the jury recommendation of life imprisonment; and others who in fact were minors when the crimes were committed. Some are mentally retarded, and others borderline; still others give every appearance of being psychotic or severely mentally deranged. Many were convicted on the plea-bargained testimony of an alleged co-committer of the crime.

While engaging in the public debate in Florida, it has been the practice of the bishops to oppose the death penalty outright, calling instead for the State to use only its available alternative, life *without* parole. Florida's law originally allowed for a sentence of death, or life imprisonment with no opportunity of parole *for 25 years*. In 1994, this law was amended to provide for death, or life imprisonment *without any parole whatsoever*. This is a fact not well known.

A 1998 Florida poll found that 63% of Floridians support the death penalty, but that support would drop dramatically if voters could be assured that those convicted would be locked-up forever, with no chance of parole. Just 50% of those polled would support the death penalty if life without parole were a certainty. Another 44% would favor banning the death penalty under those circumstances, with 6%

undecided.[17] If nothing else, this shows clearly that support for capital punishment in Florida is not nearly so great as policy makers seem to think. It also suggests that those who have engaged the debate have made at least some progress.

Abolition of the law will not be realized anytime soon, however, and engaging the debate must involve interim measures, which will limit the harm inherent in the death penalty and lessen the negative consequences. Presently, several opportunities for this exist, but this kind of change will not come easily, regardless of the apparent merits.

Pursuing Incremental Change

During the Florida Legislature's January 2000 Special Session on the death penalty, lethal injection was adopted as an alternative to the electric chair for execution in this state. Also enacted were new provisions to accelerate inmate appeals.

The Florida Catholic bishops spoke out against both of these measures and, through the Florida Catholic Conference, gave testimony to the Florida Commission on Capital Cases, whose task it was to make recommendations on this legislation:

> *Our Catholic position in opposition to the death penalty has been stated many times. Nations all over the world have been acting to put an end to the death penalty, including nearly all those in this western hemisphere and Europe. Even recently liberated countries in Eastern Europe have abolished this practice. Amnesty International and the American Bar Association have called for a moratorium, along with other secular entities. The United Nations has called for abolition. It is our sincere hope that Florida will start moving in this direction. We have repeatedly affirmed the right and duty of the state to protect society and punish criminals; we urge a consensus among policy makers, the executive and judicial branches, as well as all Floridians to-*

---

17 *Orlando Sentinel,* Mason Dixon Poll, April 1998.

ward Florida's alternative to death, that of life imprisonment with no opportunity for parole.

On *lethal injection*, the Conference offered the following statement:

It is the killing of persons to which we object, thus the means by which it is done will not change our view. Just as there is no method of committing murder, which may be sanctioned, there is no method of execution that does not serve to perpetuate the cycle of violence and promote a sense of vengeance in our culture. Lethal injection is a corruption and exploitation of medical technology. It involves a medical procedure, requires medical training in order to administer, and requires medical knowledge in order to prepare the drugs involved. Moreover, lethal injection is a violation of the Hippocratic Oath. It may be easier for some in our society to accept, but the taking of life, even if guilty, should not be acceptable. The sacredness of human life is not forfeited by human wrongdoing.

Further, the Conference noted that the American Medical Association's Code of Medical Ethics states:

A physician, as a member of a profession dedicated to preserving life when there is hope of doing so, should not be a participant in a state execution. In the case where the method of execution is lethal injection, the following actions by the physician would also constitute physician participation in execution: selecting injection sites; starting intravenous lines as a port for a lethal injection device; prescribing, preparing, administering, or supervising injection drugs or their doses or types; inspecting, testing, or maintaining lethal injection devices; and consulting with or supervising lethal injection personnel.

On the question of *accelerating appeals*, the Conference gave this testimony:

The proposal to speed up and impose time limits on post-conviction appeals is cause for grave concern. We understand that the dual track provision has created chaos in other states where some have now abandoned it. The Florida Legislature has firsthand and recent ex-

perience with persons who have spent many years on death row, had death warrants issued, followed by court ordered stays, later to be found innocent and released. News accounts in Florida have surfaced in excess of 20 of these cases, the highest incidence nationally. Since 1976, there are reports of more than 100 death row reversals nationwide, some very close to scheduled executions. In some Florida cases, the state has rightfully paid these former prisoners substantial sums for wrongful prosecution.

It is a frightening prospect that we would wrongfully kill an innocent person because an expedited appeal precluded critical information from being considered. Benjamin Franklin is credited with saying, "It is better a hundred persons should escape than one innocent person should suffer." In a state where as many as 60% of death sentences are reversed, how can we in good conscience insist on speeding up executions? On this basis alone, we would support a moratorium while this system, that all agree is in need of repair, be deliberately and carefully reviewed, something not really practical in a three-day special session.

The conference noted that on December 6, 1999, after an exhaustive study of the "collective wisdom and moral insights" of Judaism and Catholicism, the National Council of Synagogues and the National Conference of Catholic Bishops issued a joint statement entitled, "To End the Death Penalty," a portion of which is particularly on point:

In biblical times, capital punishment was a search for justice when justice seemed impossible to reach. As the Rabbis did years ago when they considered the use of the death penalty, let us take time to ask ourselves some relevant questions. Is justice reached when we are taking a chance of killing an innocent person? Is justice reached when we are discriminating against our minorities in our death sentences? See that justice is done, the prophet Zechariah proclaims.

Though the pleas of the bishops were largely unheeded, new issues arose during the Special Session. These included:

- an openness by legislators to consideration of banning the execution of mentally retarded persons;
- racial disparity in application of the death penalty; and
- interest by at least some lawmakers in requiring a unanimous jury recommendation for death.

The Florida Senate did pass a bill during the session to ban execution of the mentally retarded, but the House failed to follow suit. In an effort to appease lawmakers toward the end of the Special Session, Governor Bush, through Executive Order, appointed a Task Force on Capital Cases specifically to look at the issues of racial disparity in death sentences and mental retardation. The Florida Catholic Conference, speaking on behalf of the bishops, also urged their consideration of legislation to require a unanimous jury recommendation for a death sentence.

In testimony before the Task Force, the Florida Catholic Conference offered the following testimony in these areas:

> *Racism in Application of the Death Penalty. Any criminal penalty, and especially the death penalty, must be based on justice. Our entire constitutional, legal and civic system is based upon it and our civilization demands it. There are several studies and recent statistics that show a decided bias in application of the death penalty against murderers of whites and not blacks. The Florida Supreme Court Racial and Ethnic Bias Study Commission Report (December 1991) clearly documents that "defendants who kill Whites are more likely to be sentenced to death than defendants who kill African Americans." According to the study, ". . .the odds of a death sentence for those who kill White victims are approximately 3.4 times higher. . ." Other studies, which are available to the Task Force, also demonstrate this finding. Dr. Michael Radelet, a nationally renowned scholar and Chair of the Sociology Department at the University of*

Florida, has documented through an empirical study that racial factors affect the administration of the death penalty.

Banning Executions of the Mentally Retarded. Numerous surveys and polls indicate that a majority of Americans overwhelmingly oppose applying the death penalty on defendants who are mentally retarded. (See "Mental Retardation and the Death Penalty: Current Status of Exemption Legislation," by Keyes and Edwards, MPDLR, Sept-Oct. 1997). In Florida, polls indicated 71% opposed extending the death penalty to people with mental retardation. (See Cambridge Survey Research. Amnesty International, "An Analysis of Political Attitudes Toward the Death Penalty in Florida," May 1986.) Moreover, every other state poll taken shows between 70%-75% oppose executing the mentally retarded; this same consensus is reflected in positions held by the American Bar Association, the American Association on Mental Retardation, and the Association for Retarded Citizens.

According to the American Association on Mental Retardation, "Mental retardation refers to significantly sub-average general intellectual functioning existing concurrently with deficits in adaptive behavior and manifested during the developmental period." There exists consensus in those states that have banned capital punishment that a person with an IQ of 70 or less is mentally retarded. Just as we do not hold children responsible for criminal acts as adults, we should not hold others to a standard beyond their mental capacity. We do not suggest that such persons cannot tell right from wrong, or that they should not be held responsible. But the death penalty is the most extreme sentence available, and if we must have it, it should be reserved for the highest degree of blame. We strongly urge the Task Force to follow the example of 13 other states and Congress in outlawing capital punishment for the mentally retarded. (Note: Florida enacted a ban in 2001.)

Requiring a Unanimous Jury Verdict for Death. Among states in which juries decide sentencing, only Alabama, Delaware and Florida allow non-unanimous jury recommendations. All other death penalty states require a unanimous jury verdict for sentencing of death. In Florida, a simple 7-5 majority can yield a death sentence; a jury's recommendation of life in prison can be overridden by a judge to impose a death sentence. (Note: Thirty-eight states have the death penalty. Thirty-three have jury sentencing; the remaining five have sentences decided by a judge.) In Florida 60%-70% of death sentences are reversed on appeal (in excess of 70% in both 1998 and 1999).

Alexis de Tocqueville said, "The institution of the jury places the real direction of society in the hands of the governed and not in that of the government. He who punishes the criminal is the real master of society." As long as the death penalty is to continue in our state, the jury's role of "conscience of the community" should be strengthened and preserved. Requiring a unanimous jury verdict would undoubtedly result in two salutary effects on Florida's death penalty cases: fewer death sentences would be handed down, and the rate of death sentence reversals would substantially decrease. Further, the dilemma of life-to-death override would be largely eliminated.

In Florida, trial judges in well over a hundred cases have rejected juries' recommendations of life imprisonment. The Florida Supreme Court ruled in Tedder v. State that jury recommendations of life imprisonment may be overridden by the judge only in those rare instances where "virtually no reasonable person could differ" that death should be imposed in the case. The override provision, originally thought by many as positive since it could offer death-to-life override, has instead minimized the historical role of juries as voice of the community. Moreover, it has been hugely expensive for the state in that it has resulted in relatively few affirmed death sentences. A reputation for fairness and justice is in jeopardy with our override system. The jury is the only protection against the arbitrariness of the judge, however rare it may be. We urge the Task Force include a recommendation for unanimous jury verdict in its final report.

CONCLUSION

John Paul II, in his apostolic exhortation, *Ecclesia in America*, speaks directly to the Church in America:

> *I cannot fail to mention the unnecessary recourse to the death penalty when other 'bloodless means' are sufficient to defend human lives against an aggressor and to protect public order and the safety of persons. Today, given the means at the state's disposal to deal with crime and control those who commit it, and without abandoning all hope of their redemption, the cases where it is absolutely necessary to do away with an offender are now very rare, even non-existent practically.*[18]

Support for the death penalty is driven by fear of crime and the horror at so many lives lost through the most awful criminal violence. We must resist the common thinking that only by taking a murderer's life can justice be served.

The Church and its members must reach out to those who are today suffering because of loss from these violent crimes, even though we cannot fully appreciate their struggle and recurring pain. More must be done by our churches and communities to give comfort and care to these grieving families. Florida's bishops have instituted committees in each diocese to develop ministries that can reach out to victims of violent crimes. We must look for ways to help them resist the typical desire for revenge against those who have committed such terrible wrongs. Such revenge only feeds a climate of violence and mistakenly sees killing as a solution to this problem. Just as the teachings of the Church cannot accept abortion as a solution to unwanted or unplanned pregnancy, or assisted suicide as a solution to severe pain or depression, neither can we accept the death penalty as the solution to violence or murder.

---

18 John Paul II, Apostolic Exhortation, *Ecclesia in America*, 1999, No. 63, p. 104.

3

PHILOSOPHICAL SCHOOLS JUSTIFYING THE DEATH PENALTY

GARY FEINBERG, PH.D.
Professor of Criminal Justice
Saint Thomas University, Miami Gardens, Florida

Advocates of capital punishment generally pledge allegiance to either or both of two general schools of philosophy that define the social purpose of punishment in general, though each of these schools has it own internal variants.

Two Philosophical Schools

The first of these philosophical schools of punishment derives from classical criminology and is known variously as the "revenge school," the "retributive school," or the "just deserts school." Although each of these variously designated names reflects a slightly but importantly nuanced difference (identified and discussed later), in each instance the main goal of punishment is expressive rather than instrumental. Expressive punishment articulates the moral outrage of the community. Concomitantly, it reflects an emotive sense of moral righteousness and respectability that is grounded in Judeo-Christian thought. The action, however defined, that elicits capital punishment has so shocked society, so challenged its very existence that it screams out in a mélange of pain, grief, anguish, fear, and even terror. Such deep feelings were especially visible, for example, in the aftermath of 9/11 as the nation shuddered in collective horror at the tangible threat to its peace and security. In essence, capital punishment constitutes society's version of renting one's clothes at the tragic loss of a loved one or flailing one's arms about when in total despair.

Equally, capital punishment expresses society's total unwillingness to tolerate certain forbidden behavior. It is an announcement to all that something greater than a law has been breached. When laws are broken, the deviant behavior involved may be seriously dysfunctional to the society, but it typically falls short of threatening its very existence. Since the breaking of a law may temporarily disrupt society in a serious way, it typically meets with fines, corporal punishment and/or imprisonment. But capital punishment signifies that the offender has violated more than a law; he or she has violated a taboo. The proscribed norm in the case of a taboo is so strongly ingrained that even the thought of it is repulsive, like murder or treason. Consequently, the breaking of a taboo evokes from society an even more serious or absolute form of rejection. And, capital punishment is the quintessential form of absolute rejection.

Considerations such as preventing the offending individual from committing additional offenses or deterring others from criminal behavior in the future are irrelevant here. Instead, the focus is on an expressive response to the inherent evil nature of the offense, its desecration of the social order, and its jeopardy to the vital moral underpinnings of the society.

The second school derives from modern utilitarian philosophy and is more rationally calculating in character. It is traditionally known as the "deterrence school," but two forms of deterrence are distinguished within this school. One is 'specific deterrence" and the second is "general deterrence." In both instances, emphasis is on the ability of the punitive sanction to function as a tool to prevent or reduce the likelihood of future offenses.

Revenge Variant of the Expressive School

The revenge school, based on ancient human philosophical traditions, argues that capital punishment is retaliation by society for a crime committed against it. The pain imposed by the state in its corporate capacity is seen as the civic counterpart of the individual's natural instinct for revenge. This recapitulates an earlier time when victims could and would inflict upon their attackers the same or similar kind of crime as that suffered by them. It claims to derive its authority from the ancient Code of Hammurabi and subsequent Judeo-Christian teachings as expressed in the Bible and known as the doctrine of *lex talionis*, i.e., "an eye for an eye, a tooth for a tooth…"

It is important to comprehend, however, that the doctrine of an "eye for an eye" in Mosaic Law was understood at its inception to be a law of justice and not hatred, a law of equity and not revenge. It enjoined that a fair and equitable relation must occur between the crime and the punishment. It translates as "measure for measure," i.e. one eye for one eye, not two; one tooth for one tooth, not ten teeth for one tooth; one life for one life, not a whole family for one life, and so one. Furthermore, the doctrine assumes all citizens are equal before the law and that the injuries of each be evaluated according to the same standard. Ultimately, it deems the eye of the nobleman to be worth the same as the eye of the poorest subject.

Interestingly, more learned scholars are quick to point out that the doctrine of an eye for an eye was merely metaphorical. In practice it meant that causing the loss of an eye or hand required the offender to compensate the victim or victim's family financially in terms of the economic value of loss suffered. As Hertz (1961) observes, "The literal application of 'an eye for an eye, tooth for a tooth' was excluded in Rabbinic Law; and there is no instance in Jewish history of its literal application ever being carried out." Further, as already noted, the doctrine sought to end escalating and brutal vendettas where the punishment brought about by the vengeance seeker often exceeded the nature of the injury done to him or her by the offender. It thus promoted a more moral order and reduced the extensive wanton brutality that was practiced in the name of justice. This dimension was recognized in the writings of St. Augustine and later augmented by such pioneers of international law as Hugo Grotius and Jean Bodin. It is also true, however, that the one crime for which fiscal compensation could not serve as an alternative remedy is murder. As the Bible says, "ye shall make no ransom for the life of the murderer that is guilty of death" (Numbers 35: 31).

Today the concept of revenge as a legitimization of capital punishment has fallen into disrepute in both academic circles and the public arena, with one important and interesting exception. Advocates express the belief that failure to apply capital punishment for a crime like murder could result in vengeance seeking by the family and friends of the victim. This, in turn, could produce a spate of private lynchings, escalating the number of additional offenses and provoking further retaliation in a never ending and expanding cycle of murders and vendettas. Alternatively, it is argued, without state-imposed capital punishment, victims or their relatives may refuse to make complaint or to offer testimony, thereby handicapping the state in dealing with criminals.

Retribution & Just-Deserts Variants of the Expressive School

Those who advocate capital punishment as a form of retribution distinguish themselves from those who speak of capital punishment as a form of revenge by pointing out that their position emphasizes doing justice and following due process. Moreover, they see the application and administration of capital punishment as something objectively and dispassionately applied and thus quite different from subjectively and emotionally driven acts of revenge.

Here punishment is perceived as deserved by an offender who acts willfully in violating the moral basis of peace and order in the society.

Correlatively, society is seen as having the moral right and duty to punish the guilty.

In this argument, society's right to punish is given by the fact that the integrity of its moral order has been challenged; it has the duty to punish because not to do so denies the very meaning of crime and renders the concept of moral responsibility meaningless. In the case of capital punishment, for retributionists the penalty matches the severity of the crime (e.g. murder, treason). In this way it gives meaning to the term justice. Indeed, for advocates of capital punishment, matching the offense to the penalty is the very essence of doing justice.

These advocates scorn the utilitarian objective of deterrence as having nothing to do with justice *qua* justice. Consequently, they are disinterested in any research related to either the pros or cons of capital punishment as a mechanism for deterring crime. For them, deterrence objectives are irrelevant to the quest of doing justice. The latter is simply a matter of linking the level of moral outrage experienced by the community to the severity of the punishment.

Where that moral outrage so shocks the collective conscience of the community, capital punishment as the most severe penalty is what constitutes "just deserts." Moreover, failure to apply the penalty to those who violated the law, it is argued, would serve only to mock those who respect the deeply held moral values of society upon which the law is based (Barlow, 2001).

SUPPORTERS & CRITICS OF RETRIBUTION

Support for the retribution school comes clearly from the United States Supreme Court. In *Gregg v. Georgia* (1976), the Court expressed the belief that, while retribution may not be the most popular basis for legitimating punishment for crimes, it is not a forbidden objective and it is in keeping with our notion of human dignity. "Indeed, the decision that capital punishment may be the appropriate sanction in extreme cases is an expression of the community's belief that certain crimes are themselves so grievous an affront to humanity that the only adequate response may be the penalty of death" (*Gregg v. Georgia*, 1976).

The Supreme Court wrote of the instinct for retribution as natural and feared that, if the courts refused to acknowledge it, private individuals would take the law into their own hands. "Capital punishment is at its quick an expression of the society's moral outrage" (*Gregg v., Georgia*, 1976).

This argument may seem unappealing to many, but it was an essential part of an orderly society wherein citizens were expected to rely on and to respect the formal legal procedures, and not seek self-redress for wrongs done to them. In addition, as Sue Titus Reid (2001) observes, it appears that the Supreme Court was relying more and more on the concept of retribution as a justification for capital punishment due to the lack of more recent empirical studies supporting this sanction as a successful deterrent.

Supporters of this school also include British Protestant Christian apologist C.S. Lewis (1971) who wrote:

> *The concept of desert is the only connecting link between punishment and justice. It is only as deserved or undeserved that a sentence can be just or unjust ... We may properly ask whether it is likely to deter others and to reconform the criminal. But neither of these two last questions is a question about justice. There is no sense in talking about a just deterrent or a just cure; we demand of a deterrent not whether it is just but whether it will deter. We demand of a cure not whether it is just but whether it succeeds. (As quoted in Schmalleger, 1996).*

Von Hirsch (1976) summarizes the supportive conclusion of an elite group of educators and lawyers researching the subject of punishment when he offers that the only just system of punishment is one based on retribution. Here offenders are seen as having free will, acting with volition, pursuing goals, and enjoying choice. Consequently, they should be considered and treated as fully responsible for their behavior.

Some contemporary secular critics who challenge retribution as the legitimate objective of capital punishment may be found especially in leftist camps and are often associated with what may be called the "radical school" of criminology. These critics contend that criminal-law violators are themselves victims of an unjust society. They point out that those who are typically subject to capital punishment are inevitably drawn from among the poor, the disenfranchised, and minority classes. In their argument, the accused are depicted as victims of an unfair distribution of the nation's wealth, of its discriminatory and exploitative opportunity structure, and of its materialistic and egotistic source of self worth.

Capital punishment, in turn, is viewed as one more way for those who control the means of production to maintain their positions of privilege in the country and to protect their unfair advantages. These critics also challenge the thesis that such offenders have free will, act with volition, or enjoy choice. Rather, they see responsibility for crime as resting with those in power who have unfairly and unjustly treated certain segments of society, alienating and isolating them so as to maximize and protect their own economic advantages. Among those giving intellectual voice to such "radical" or critical views of the retributionists school are noted sociologists Richard Quinney (1979) and William Chambliss (1988).

In addition, such writers frequently support their position by citing numerous statistical studies demonstrating that minorities – especially Blacks, Hispanics, the poor, and the disenfranchised – are significantly over-represented on death row and in the nation's execution chambers. (See, for example, Death Row, USA, Winter 2000.) These allegations of institutionalized racism within the justice system, and the correlative challenge that capital cases discriminate against minorities, are powerful criticisms which are difficult to ignore. Indeed, in several instances they have effectively impressed the U.S. Supreme Court. (See, for example, *Furman v. Georgia*, 1972.)

In response, advocates of the death penalty acknowledge the empirical reality that blacks, the poor, the disenfranchised and other minorities are disproportionately selected onto death penalty rosters while Whites, the rich, and the powerful seem socially immunized from this ultimate form of punishment. In defense, however, they argue that the disproportionate vulnerability of minorities to the death penalty does not make them any less guilty. Nor should the fact that Whites or wealthy individuals escape the death penalty mean that these others should not get the punishment they deserve (Van der Haag, 1991).

Instrumental School of Deterrence

The second major contemporary school of thought that justifies capital punishment is based on the modern philosophy of utilitarianism and is known as the "deterrence school." Its central thesis argues that punishment is merited as a necessary, effective, and efficient means to prevent unwanted behavior, including crime, and in the case of capital punishment, murder or treason. In addition, this school argues, the threat and actuality of punishment is a rational and calculated means for improving social behavior. For this school, punishment in general becomes a device for educating and reforming actual criminals while at the same time frightening would-be criminals into refraining from such behavior. The goal of deterrence theory is to prevent future criminal behavior rather than to seek retribution from the offender.

Originating in the works of such 18th Century utilitarian philosophers as Cesare Beccaria and Jeremy Bentham, the theory assumes that perpetrators have free will. Furthermore, it assumes that they rationally choose their actions so as to maximize pleasure by carefully weighing the costs and benefits likely to accrue from them. In this perspective, the threat of punishment compels people toward conformity with the law, since they fear physical and material deprivation as well as the loss of membership in the social order.

But the theory ignores the reality that people often behave out of impulse, passion, or habit, that is, without rationally calculated planning or reflection. Moreover, individuals frequently lack information needed to make an accurate rational assessment of the risks and potential benefits of a given course of action. Indeed, even the hedonistic philosophical assumption underlying the so-called "calculus of deterrence" has been challenged for several generations.

This is not to say that fear of punishment cannot deter. It certainly can. The weight of scholarly research on the subject, however, points out that for deterrence to occur the punishment must be both swift and certain (Beccaria, 1764, 1963; Grasmick and McLaughlin, 1978). It is quickly evident that these requirements of swiftness and certainty compromise due process protections so pivotal to a civilized society, for example, the right to notice and hearing, the right to call witnesses on one's own behalf, the right to cross examine prosecutorial witnesses, the right to appeal, the right to be free from forced confessions, the right to defense counsel, as well as the right to be treated as innocent until proven guilty. The real issue, then, concerns our ability and willingness to live free and constructive lives in a society that rejects such due process protections in preference for swift and certain punishments.

One branch of the deterrence school posits capital punishment functions as an absolute "specific deterrent." Simply stated, by executing the convicted murderer or similar offender who shocks the collective conscience of the society and jeopardizes the society's very existence, it is guaranteed that this particular individual will not repeat his or her offense and harm society again. The deterrence is specific to the particular offender.

A second branch is known as the "general deterrence" variant. It takes the position that punishment of one individual for committing a crime serves to deter others from committing a similar act in the future. For this branch, capital punishment is justified as a way of reinforcing the idea that certain behaviors are absolutely prohibited by the society and that anyone who violates laws proscribing such behavior will suffer the extreme penalty. According to its proponents, deterrence thus serves an important moral affirmation for the public at large, stifles the growth of criminalistic ideologies, and effects what Andenaes (1974) calls the "moral or socio-pedagogical influence of punishment."

SUPPORTERS & CRITICS OF DETERRENCE

Advocates of capital punishment who cite it as a specific deterrence focus on the dangers to society continually posed by the individual offender, should he or she be allowed to live. This includes the threat they would present to the life and well being of prison administrators, guards, and even other inmates, should they merely be incarcerated. Minimally, it is contended, holding out the threat of capital punishment serves to protect such individuals from irrepressibly violent offenders who would otherwise have nothing to lose by committing additional murders.

Those who espouse capital punishment as a means of general deterrence contend that executing certain criminal-law violators will extinguish similar motivations toward criminal behavior in other members of the community. They frequently conduct and cite research to support their position that capital punishment for certain crimes deters others from committing similar acts. Some of these studies compare murder rates in states that have capital punishment with those rates in contiguous states that do not have capital punishment. Others cite temporal studies comparing murder rates within a given state during years when capital punishment is in effect and during years when it has been abolished. Additional studies have been done to address the question of whether or not well-publicized executions produce at least short-term reductions in homicide, especially in those areas close to where the executions are taking place.

Critics of the general deterrence school cite a robust literature of empirical studies that counter the position that states employing capital punishment enjoy reduced rates of crime when compared to other states that do not have capital punishment. One major review of the research done several decades ago evaluating the effect of the death penalty as a deterrent to murder concluded that, although a few studies (e.g., Ehrlich, 1975) did support the notion of capital punishment having a deterrent effect, the evidence to date was inadequate for drawing any substantive conclusions (Blumstein, Cohen, and Nagin, 1978). As Paternoster (1991) more recently observed, despite years of research aimed at revealing a general deterrent effect of capital punishment, and regardless of the diverse methodologies and statistical tests used, the weight of scholarly empirical evidence tends to reject any hypothesis that capital punishment somehow reduces the likelihood of murders being committed.

Nevertheless, abolitionists remain on the defensive. Invariably they must joust against those who argue that the presence of capital punishment prevents "untold numbers" of murders from being committed. Unfortunately, this figure is more asserted than validated since it is impossible to verify. Murders that have never occurred cannot be counted.

Perhaps surprisingly to some, there is even a body of literature arguing that the use of capital punishment actually increases rather than decreases the incidence of homicide. Bowers and Pierce (1980), for example, found that an average of two additional homicides above the normal expectation occurred in the month following an execution. This led them to espouse what has come to be known as the "brutalization effect" of capital punishment. Here the argument is made that certain unstable types are actually spurred on to commit murder by seeing the state use lethal violence to effect its own ends.

Critics who reject capital punishment in general, including both revenge theory and specific (or individual) as well as general deterrence theory, are quick to identify instances where innocent individuals have been executed. Such critics are repeating the historic challenge of Voltaire (Francois Marie Arouet), an acerbic eighteenth-century French philosopher who challenged capital punishment and embarrassed French state authorities by aggressively demonstrating that innocent persons had been regularly executed by the French state for crimes they did not commit.

A more contemporary version of this argument is likely to point out that in the United States from 1973 through 1999 as many as 84 death row inmates were released as wrongfully accused. Most of these releases were due to new evidence made available as a result of scientific advances, and especially the introduction of DNA testing, as well as through the tenacious efforts of journalists, professors, and activists against the death penalty, college students, and public interest lawyers. Regrettably, according to research conducted by Bedau and Radelet (1987), at least 23 others were not so fortunate, with proof of their innocence not benefiting from such evidence until their executions had already taken place.

Indeed, as recently as January 31, 2000, Governor George Ryan of Illinois, driven by the harsh reality that more of the state's death row inmates had to be released because they were wrongfully convicted (as substantiated by newly found irrefutable DNA evidence) than were actually executed since the state re-instituted the death penalty, announced a temporary halt to all such executions. Concomitantly, he commissioned a blue ribbon panel to investigate why so many wrongful death penalty incarcerations are happening despite an abundance of so-called legal protections. Additional states are considering similar moratoriums.

Alternatively, evidence such as DNA also helps confirm the guilt of accused individuals and thereby reduces a major argument for eliminating the death penalty. Moreover, it could likely result in the reopening of old capital cases and their exemption from double jeopardy protections as previously wrongfully exonerated defendants are summoned back to court and sent to death row.

Conclusion

We have reviewed here the two major contemporary schools of philosophical argument in favor of the death penalty, as well as some of the critical challenges to these schools.

The revenge theory stems from ancient philosophical roots, while the deterrence theory is based on the modern utilitarian ethics that arose within the liberal philosophical project. Each has its supporters and detractors.

In addition, which school tends to enjoy hegemony over the other seems to vary by historical period. For instance, during much of the twentieth century both the retribution and deterrence value of punishment were largely ignored in favor of still a totally different theory, namely, rehabilitation. Then beginning with an important work by a Norwegian legal scholar, Johannes Andenaes (1952), in the mid-twentieth century interest began to reemerge in the deterrent value of punishment.

(Editors' note. As pointed out earlier, neither of these theories constituted the philosophical basis for the earlier Catholic justification of the death penalty, which was traditionally grounded in the doctrine of a community's right to self-defense. For more on the Catholic philosophical justification prior to the new development of Catholic social teaching, see among others the essay later in this volume on Thomas Aquinas by Robert Valle.)

Today, however, within the United States there is a strong political preference for the ancient retribution theory. As in biblical days, retribution has been argued once more as the only legitimate use of punishment in general and of capital punishment in particular.

This is not to discount the fact that many advocates of the death penalty do not reject the idea of deterrence in principle, but they often lament that the conditions for capital punishment to deter are absent. In particular, they point out that, in contemporary U.S. society, capital punishment is neither swift nor certain – critical prerequisites to its effective functioning as a deterrent.

(For a more detailed summary on the discussions of the retribution and deterrence schools of punishment, see Schmalleger, 1996; Reid, 2001; Barlow, 2001; Conklin, 1992).

Briefly stated, the most common arguments made in favor of the death penalty are as follows:

- It is more effective than any other penalty in deterring murder;
- It is needed to prevent private revenge and a lynch law society;
- It is the only certain penalty for murderers who are sentenced to life imprisonment, frequently secure paroles or pardons;
- It is more economical than imprisonment;
- It affirms what is morally right in society and the unforgivable gravity of murder;
- While blacks, the poor, and other minorities are disproportionately represented on death row, this itself does not make them less guilty; it only affirms that the application of capital punishment needs to overcome unfair protections of whites, the wealthy, and the empowered.

On the other hand, those who oppose capital punishment argue that:

- It is not a more effective deterrent than imprisonment;
- Its abolition does not precipitate private lynchings;
- It reduces the certainty and swiftness of punishment;
- It reduces respect for human life and thereby promotes murder;
- It produces irreparable errors of justice;
- It diminishes the morale of both inmates and staff in institu-

tions where it is implemented (See: Sutherland and Cressey, 1978);

- It discriminates against blacks, the poor, and other minorities – a variant of institutional racism.

As we continue to enter a twenty-first-century postmodern global society in which fewer and fewer nations across the planet employ capital punishment on a regular basis, philosophical arguments for and against capital punishment continue to spur an energized debate among religious scholars, criminologists, penologists, lawyers, jurists, educators, and intellectuals, as well as within the public at large.

BIBLIOGRAPHY

Andenaes, J. (1952). "General Prevention – Illusion or Reality." *Journal of Criminal Law, Criminology, and Police Science.* 43: 176-198.

___________. (1974). *Punishment and Deterrence.* Ann Arbor, Michigan: University of Michigan Press.

Barlow, H. D. (2001). *Introduction to Criminology.* 8th Edition. New York: Harper Collins.

Becarria, C. (1764, 1963). *On Crime and Punishment.* Indianapolis, Ind.: Bobbs Merrill.

Bedau, H. A. and M. L. Radelet. (1987). "Miscarriages of Justice in Potentially Capital Cases." *Stanford Law Review.* 40: 457-466.

Blumstein, A., J. Cohen, and D. Nagin (1978). *Deterrence and Incapacitation: Estimating the Effects of Criminal Sanctions on Crime Rates.* Washington, D. C.: National Academy of Sciences.

Bowers, W. J. and G. L. Pierce (1980). "Arbitrariness and Discrimination in Post-Furman Capital Statutes." *Crime and Criminology.* 26:563-635.

Chambliss, W. (1988). *Exploring Criminology.* 2nd Edition. New York: Macmillan.

Conklin, J. E. (1992). *Criminology.* 4th Edition. New York: Macmillan.

Death Row USA., Winter 2000. New York: NAACP Defense and Educational Fund, January 1, 2000, p. 1.

Ehrlich, I. (1975). "The Deterrent Effect of Capital Punishment: A Question of Life and Death." *American Economic Review.* 65:387-407.

Furman v. Georgia, (1972) 408 U.S. 238

Grasmick, H. C. & McLaughlin, S. D. (1978). "Comment: Deterrence and Social Control." *American Sociological Review* 43:272-278.

Gregg v. Georgia, (1976), 428 *U.S.* 153.

Hertz, J.H. (1961). Editor. *Pentateuch and Haftorahs*. London: The Soncino Press, Ltd.

Lewis, C.S. (1971). "The Humanitarian Theory of Punishment," in Stanley E. Grupp, ed. *Theories of Punishment.* Bloomington: University of Indiana Press, 301-308.

Quinney, R. E. (1979). *Criminology*. 2nd Edition. Boston: Little Brown.

Reid, S. T. (2001). *Crime and Criminology*. 9th Edition. New York: Holt, Rinehart and Winston.

Schmalleger, F. (1996). *Criminology Today*. Englewood Cliffs, N. J.: Prentice Hall.

Sutherland, Edwin H. and Donald R. Cressey. *Criminology*. 10th Edition. Philadelphia, Pa.: J.B. Lippincott Company.

Von Hirsch, A. (1976). *Doing Justice: The Choice of Punishments*. New York: Hill and Wang.

4

RACISM AND THE DEATH PENALTY

ROBIN LOVETT, J.D.
Assistant Professor of Social Science
Saint Thomas University, Miami Gardens, Florida

Philosophers have always been vitally interested in discussions about death. Many of them have consumed much of their speculative attention and concern with death and its implications. Socrates maintained "that the whole essence and function of philosophy is to prepare a person for death." Others have in some ways attempted to apply either magic or mysticism to the contemplation of death. Pascal mentions the paradox of trying to put death out of one's thinking and the constant preoccupation that death plays in one's ordinary routine.

While these philosophical principles may make for interesting abstract theory, for a person of color on death row the opinions of these great philosophers are less germane than the concrete and practical question of racism and the death penalty.[1]

Racism in American Society

If asked "Are you racist?" many of us would not hesitate to answer: "Of course not!" Besides wanting to answer in what is perceived to be a politically correct manner, most Americans visualize themselves

1 Death as a Constant Companion, *Time*, Nov. 12, 1965 at 52-53.

as being free from the images that are routinely associated with racism, prejudice, and bigotry. We see ourselves as fair and just individuals. We deem ourselves above and far removed from our nation's historical racially segregated past. Some of us are not hesitant to refer to ourselves as upstanding citizens.

As a gesture of utmost respect to our Creator, some of us refer to ourselves as Christians and take pride in Christianity's affirmation of equality for all humans. Yet this is a paradox in light of the fact that Sunday, the day that most Americans actually take the time out from their busy lives to reinforce their religious beliefs, seems to be the most segregated day of the week in our country. If we look in our churches, our parishes, our tabernacles, or wherever it is that we choose as our place of worship, would we be surprised to find that they do not reflect the racial makeup of our society – just like our prison – just like death row?

If you were a Christian, would this bother you? Are we to ignore the issues that are associated with race because they offend the majority of us who can't perceive that racism is alive and well in America? It is almost painful to think that Sunday in America may be truly the most segregated day of the week. We pray and speak of our love of God. We seek in our lives the presence of a God whom we have not seen. Yet we shun responsibility for our brothers and sisters. Each time a death sentence is imposed does our silence sanction the death in our society of those who were created by this same God? If we are indeed acting with a Christ-like conscience, is there a duty to consider God's philosophy in this matter?

THE SUPREME COURT, RACE, & THE DEATH PENALTY

The phenomena of racism and how it is associated with the implementation of the death penalty in the American criminal justice system is nothing new. It is a direct reflection of the inherent racism that exists in our society. In *Furman v. Georgia*, the Supreme Court had the opportunity to address the issue of "whether the death sentence, as being imposed, was administered arbitrarily and capriciously." This issue was considered especially in regards to the sentencing of blacks. In the Supreme Court's 1972 ruling in *Furman v. Georgia*, the Court responded in the affirmative, and as a result the death penalty laws were effectively thrown out nationwide.

The Supreme Court revisited its decision in its 1976 ruling in *Gregg v. Georgia.* In light of the Furman decision, Georgia law was changed. The new law mandated a bifurcated trail for capital cases. The first stage gives the criminal defendant charged with the capital offence a trail on his or her guilt or innocence, as in any other case. The second stage determines whether the death penalty is the appropriate sentence. The new law also gave one convicted an automatic appeal to the Georgia Supreme Court. The new Georgia statute was upheld, the death penalty therein reinstated.

The on-going debate as to whether capital punishment is a true deterrence to crime, if believed, still does not justify the disproportionate number of African-Americans who are awaiting execution. If we statistically contrast America's overall African-American population with the number of African-Americans on death row, we will find a disproportionate number awaiting their execution. Nor should we be at all surprised to find that the evidence supports a death penalty system that has historically been racially biased and systematically unfair to all people of color and to African-Americans in particular.

The use of the death penalty as punishment for criminals has not served its purpose. Homicide rates continue to rise, and other crimes continue to follow the same direction. Research indicates that discriminatory practices have undeniably been used. From 1973 to the present, there have been more than 48 known mistakenly planned executions that were resolved barely in time to save an innocent defendant's life. Undeniably the question arises time and time again: when will this barbaric use of punishment be banned in all states? Capital punishment does not significantly reduce crime, it is unfairly applied to certain races, and it poses the threat of killing many innocent people. Why does such a crude and useless method continue in a nation that claims to be so developed, so civilized?[2]

With this in mind, it is quite disturbing to know that, since the mid-1980s, Americans have consistently and publicly supported the death penalty by 70 to 80 percent. Is this support due in part to the complacency or lack of concern for minorities who are disproportionately represented when subjected to this ultimate form of punishment? Or could racism by those who support the death penalty be the real explanation for their strong support, or at least one of the delicate and unspoken reasons that the proponents of the death penalty carry within them?

The Supreme Court's present position on capital punishment does not fundamentally challenge the constitutionality of the death penalty, even when recently the Court agreed to decide on whether the use of the electric chair by Florida would be cruel and unusual punishment and in violation of the 8th Amendment. But a decision by the Supreme Court against the "cruel and unusual punishment" aspect of capital punishment could possibly bring attention and new interest to the plight of those on death row and may garner some support for other issues associated with the implementation of a capital sentence under our criminal justice system.

Racism in the Criminal Justice System

One way of attempting to understand racism as it pertains to capital punishment would be to examine the institutions within our criminal justice system. We should not be afraid to recognize the fact that our society allows, creates, ignores, and sometimes even supports racism. Unfortunately for these reasons, racism went long unchecked and remains deeply woven into the fabric of this country. Racism and the

---

2 Quintana, Annette (2000), "Capital Punishment: An Unreliable and Discriminatory Practice," Unpublished paper.

negative effects thereof are seen every day, especially by those adversely affected by it.

The American criminal justice system, like other systems of our society, has not truly reflected equality and justice for all. When a criminal justice system like ours is inherently biased against a particular group of people, whose fault is it? Unable to find a responsible person, these issues become easier simply to ignore.

If something does not affect us on a personal level, are our actions to be governed by the "Don't ask –don't tell rule"? If that is the case, then maybe our actions can be considered not morally wrong, just passive. If we allow ourselves to become a product of passive racism, however, we may suffer from the illusion that racial harmony and equality for all has already been achieved in this county. But our history and the evidence simply do not support this illusion. Passive racism is just as dangerous as active racism. To ignore and thereby allow the systematic, unequal, and unfair treatment of minorities in our system creates and fosters an atmosphere of inequality and prevents the progression of racial harmony in our society.

Racism and its impact on minority inmates on death row appear long before the sentencing process. To have been sentenced to death, an inmate had to have participated and to have gone through the entire American criminal justice process. Unfortunately in this process there is ample opportunity for racism to present itself. One may ask: "How is that possible?"

Let us answer that question. The American criminal justice system is comprised of three components: 1) the police; 2) the courts; and 3) corrections. Each component has individual authority, autonomy, and discretion as it functions in this system. Each component needs in turn to be examined in relation to racism.

THE POLICE COMPONENT

The initial decision to investigate a case and to pursue it as a capital offense is usually made by someone in the police department. From the investigating officer's interpretation of the events leading up to the alleged criminal activity, an offense that has the potential of becoming a capital offense may be so charged, or it may instead be charged as a first-degree felony or even a lesser offense.

Historically some argue that there has been great disparity between charges filed against non-minority offenders who had allegedly raped and/or murdered a minority victim, in contrast to charges filed against minority offenders for the same offenses allegedly committed against a non-minority victim. This contrast has left many questioning the impartiality of the criminal justice system. There are also those who indicate that, if both the alleged offender and the victim are from a minority race, the potential charges are not as strictly scrutinized. Thus the initial interaction with the criminal justice system through policing becomes critical as it relates to who will actually be criminally charged with a capital offense.

The Court Component

After the police department has completed its investigation, the second stage of interaction in the criminal justice process begins with the court process. This stage is also critical and may reveal hidden or latent effects of racism. For example, a judge, whose appointment or election to his or her judicial capacity typically is not representative of the racial makeup of the minority community, arraigns the defendant.

This in and of itself does not indicate that the defendant will be treated unfairly; however, when coupled with other inequalities in the system, this may diminish the likelihood of equal justice for this defendant. This is especially the case when frequently the defendant is indigent and counsel for the defendant is appointed directly by the judge who now sets the tone for the defendant's representation. This judge has now subconsciously set the tone for the entire trial process.

This process seldom truly affords a minority defendant the exercise of one of our basic Constitutional rights, namely, the amendment right to a jury of one's "peers." How fair would the judicial system seem to most European Americans if they were charged with a criminal offense and justice lay in the hands of twelve African American Jurors? In addition, imagine if the judge, the prosecutor, and the court-appointed counsel were also African American? If we were defendants in this situation, would the judicial system seem fair to us? In theory the answer might be "yes," but in reality for many this answer would be "no." Yet this is the plight of the many minority defendants who are processed every day through our criminal court system.

So is there impartial justice in America for the minority defendant? Or, as some minority defendants believe, is it really "just-us" in a criminal justice system badly in need of reform?

THE CORRECTIONS COMPONENT

As we see that statistically the number of those in prison in general – and on death row in particular – do not at all reflect the general population of our society, the whole process becomes particularly difficult to defend.

The U.S. Census Bureau (1999) statistical data support the discrimination argument. The findings indicate that there were 4,291 prisoners executed between the years of 1930 to 1988. When categorized by race, of those executed 2,201 were black and 1,971 were white. Given the ethnic makeup of our society, these statistics give us a painful reminder of the racial discrimination in sentencing. The Texas coalition to abolish the death penalty states that, "the death penalty is racist; it indicates that 42% of those in death row are African American, although blacks are just 13% of its population."

In summary, the disparity in sentencing as to the death penalty will continue to exist as long as "we the people" look the other way when our corporate board rooms, our neighborhoods, our school and our churches reflect anything other than the racial and ethnic make up of our communities. Equal Opportunity under the law will never change the heart, the soul, and the mind of so many of us.

Bibliography

Death as a Constant Companion, Time, Nov. 12, 1965 at 52-53.

Furman v. Georgia, 408 U.S. 238, 92 S.CT 2726, 33 L. Ed. 2nd 346(1972).

Gregg v. Georgia, 418 U.S. 153, 96 S.CT 2909, 49 L. Ed. 2nd 859 (1976).

Quintana, Annette (2000), "Capital Punishment: An Unreliable and Discriminatory Practice," Unpublished paper.

5

A CATHOLIC LAWYER REFLECTS ON THE DEATH PENALTY

RICHARD R. MCCORMACK, J.D.
Attorney at Law, Private Practice

The original version of this paper was presented as part of the author's course work for a master's degree in Pastoral Ministry at Saint Thomas University in Miami Gardens, Florida.

A Haunting Question

After the convicted killer was put to death in Florida on August 25, 2000 by lethal injection, the murdered victim's mother who witnessed the execution was quoted as saying, "It was too humane; I would like to go back to Old Sparky."[1]

Suppose that an innocent seven-year old girl is repeatedly raped, sodomized and brutally beaten to death. Then suppose that the killer is positively identified by state-of-the-art DNA testing, arrested, and contemptuously confesses without remorse to the murder. Now imagine that the murdered girl is your granddaughter. How would you feel about the death penalty?

In another and real notorious case, do you suppose that there would have been any reluctance by the family members of the victims of

---

1 http: www.sptimes.com/News/082600/State/Witness_to_execution_shtml

the *Shoah* to request the death penalty for Adolf Hitler (had he survived), or for the hijackers of the aircraft that crashed into the World Trade Center buildings in New York City on September 11 (had they not also been killed in the event)?

Similarly, I often ask myself: "Would I object to the use of the death penalty if one of my family members was one of the 168 innocent people murdered by Timothy McVeigh in Oklahoma?"

Arguments concerning the morality of imposing death as punishment for crimes are not new. Compare the statement made in 458 B.C.E. by Aeschylus in *Libation Bearers*, "It is but law that when the red drops have been spilled upon the ground they cry aloud for fresh blood," with that made in 408 B.C.E. by Euripides in *Orestes*, "Our ancestors ... purged their guilt by banishment, not death. And by so doing, they stopped that endless vicious cycle of murder and revenge."[2]

A Personal Experience

It is easy to be indifferent about the imposition of the death penalty when you are not personally involved. The closest I came to having to make that decision was when I was called to criminal jury duty about six years ago. It was a case involving a gay man who came upon his lover engaged in a sexual act with another man. The gay man shot them both and they died. He was charged by the State with first-degree murder. There was no doubt that he was guilty of the crime. The only issue was whether he was going to be executed.

The attorneys' questions sought to elicit our attitudes and beliefs concerning the imposition of the death penalty. Up until that moment, I never really thought much about it. After all, the victims and the accused murderers were always unknowns.

---

2 David L. Bender and Bruno Leone, eds., *The Death Penalty: Opposing Viewpoints* (2d ed.) Greenhaven Press (San Diego, CA 1991), p. 12.

Yet, sitting in the jury box and being questioned about my beliefs about the death penalty made me realize that I may be called to judge whether another human lives or dies. The thought sobered my cavalier attitude. My responses to the questioning by the attorneys became very deliberate and measured.

I was not picked to serve on the jury. I later learned that the prosecutor had sought to have me excused for cause, arguing that my responses demonstrated that I was predisposed against the death penalty. Actually, I did not believe that the death penalty was necessarily warranted under the facts of that case. Would I have thought differently had it involved the rape and brutal murder of a mother of three children?

Since then I have been contemplating what it means to be human, the inherent dignity of humans: "Then God said: 'Let us make man in our image, after our likeness ... God created man in his image; in the divine image he created him; male and female he created them.'"[3]

I am engaged in the Outreach ministry at my parish. It is not difficult to talk about the dignity of life and our baptismal commitment that calls us to feed the poor, give drink to the thirsty, welcome the stranger, clothe the naked, and care for the sick.[4] It is quite another matter to honor the commitment to visit those in prison[5] or to forgive a mass murderer. Yet perhaps recognizing the inherent human dignity of a mass murderer is part of also affirming the human dignity of all humanity.

Ancient Roots of the Death Penalty

The death penalty has been part of the human condition for thousands of years. During approximately the eighteenth century B.C.E., the Code of King Hammurabi of Babylon codified the death penalty

---

3 Genesis 1:26-27.

4 Matthew 25:31-46.

5 Matthew 25:36.

for about 25 different crimes.[6] The death penalty was also part of the fourteenth century B.C.E. Hittite Code, as well as the seventh century B.C.E. Draconian Code of Athens. In the fifth century B.C.E. Roman Law of the Twelve Tablets, death sentences were carried out by such means as beating to death, burning alive, drowning and crucifixion. In the tenth century C.E., Britain employed hanging as the usual method for execution. [7]

Much later in Britain, it is estimated that under the sixteenth century reign of Henry VIII as many as 72,000 people may have been executed by hanging, burning at the stake, beheading, boiling and drawing and quartering. By the 1700s, 222 crimes were punishable by death in Britain.[8]

It was urged in Britain at the time that punishment for criminals should remain severe and painful (such as whipping them to death instead of merely hanging them at the gallows), and that keeping the death penalty as a very real threat was the only way to stop people from committing heinous and violent crimes.[9]

> *If Death then be due to a Man, who surreptitiously steals the Value of Five Shillings (as it is made by a late Statute) surely He who puts me in fear of my Life, and breaks the King's peace, and it may be,*

---

6 Death Penalty Information Center, "History of the Death Penalty: Part I," www.deathpenaltyinfo.org/ history2.html, citing L. Randa, ed., *Society's Final Solution: A History and Discussion of the Death Penalty* (University Press of America, 1997).

7 Ibid.

8 Ibid.

9 David L. Bender and Bruno Leone, eds. Death Penalty Information Center, "History of the Death Penalty: Part I." www.deathpenaltyinfo.org/history2.html, citing L. Randa, ed., *Society's Final Solution: A History and Discussion of the Death Penalty* (University Press of America, 1997). The Death Penalty: Opposing Viewpoints (2d ed.) Greenhaven Press (San Diego, CA 1991), p. 17, referring to *Hanging Not Punishment Enough for Murtherers, Highway Men, and House-Breakers*, London: A. Balwin, 1701.

murders me at last, and burns my House, deserves another sort of Censure; and if the one must die, the other should be made to feel himself die...[10]

The noted early liberal philosopher and economist, John Stuart Mill, who served as a member of the British Parliament from 1865 to 1868, advocated political and social reforms such as the emancipation for women, and the development of farm cooperatives and labor organizations. During a debate in Parliament on April 21, 1868, however, Mill argued for lesser penalties for crimes such as theft, but urged that society must retain the death penalty for crimes of murder. He reasoned:

> ... *the influence of a punishment is not to be estimated by its effect on [the hardened criminals], so to speak, at all times within the sight of the gallows, do grow to care less about it; as, to compare good things with bad, an old soldier is not much affected by the chance of dying in battle. I can afford to admit all that is often said about the indifference of professional criminals to the gallows ... But the efficacy of a punishment which acts principally through the imagination, is chiefly to be measured by the impression it makes on those who are still innocent: by the horror which surrounds the first prompting of guilt; the restraining influence it exercises over the beginning of the thought which, if indulged, would become a temptation; the check which it exerts over the gradual declension towards the state – never suddenly attained – in which crime no longer revolts, and punishment no longer terrified.*[11]

British law carried over to America. The first recorded execution occurred in the Jamestown colony of Virginia in 1608. It is reported that laws were enacted in 1612 that required the death penalty for

---

10 Ibid.

11 David L. Bender and Bruno Leone, eds., *The Death Penalty: Opposing Viewpoints*, 2nd ed. (San Diego, CA: Greenhaven Press 1991), pp. 27-33, quoting from John Stuart Mill, Hansard's *Parliamentary Debate*, 3rd Series, London: April 21, 1868.

minor offenses such as killing chickens, trading with Indians, or stealing grapes. The Duke's Laws of 1665 enacted in the New York colony allowed death as a punishment for such offenses as denying the "true God" or striking one's mother or father. [12]

Modern Abolitionism & the U.S. Experience

An Abolitionist movement arose against the death penalty only in modern times. The Abolitionists were influenced by an essay written in 1767 by the Italian Cesare Beccaria and entitled *On Crimes and Punishment.* Beccaria asserted that there was no justification for the state's taking of human life:

> *The death of a citizen cannot be necessary, but in one case. When, though deprived of his liberty, he has such power and connections as may endanger the security of the nation; when his existence may produce a dangerous revolution in the established form of government. But even in this case, it can only be necessary when a nation is on the verge of recovering or losing its liberty; or in times of absolute anarchy, when the disorders themselves hold the place of laws. But in a reign of tranquility; in a form of government approved by the united wishes of the nation; in a state well fortified from enemies without, and supported by strength within, and opinion, perhaps more efficacious; where all power is lodged in the hands of a true sovereign; where riches can purchase pleasures and not authority, there can be no necessity for taking away the life of a subject.*[13]

Through the Abolitionist movement, certain states in the U.S. began enacting laws that limited the application of the death penalty to certain egregious crimes such as first degree murder and treason. Afterwards, Wisconsin and Rhode Island banned the death penalty for all crimes, whose practice, by the end of the nineteenth century, was

---

12 Ibid.

13 Ibid, p. 22, quoting from Cesare Beccaria, *An Essay on Crimes and Punishments*, originally published in London by F. Newberry, 1775.

followed by Portugal, Ecuador, Brazil, Netherlands, and Venezuela. In view of the Abolitionist movement and in an apparent effort to make the death penalty more palatable, other states began enacting laws that made the death penalty discretionary. By 1863 most mandatory capital punishment laws in the United States had been abolished. [14]

Criminals were generally executed by hanging or firing squad. States began developing different means for executing their criminals. New York introduced the electric chair in 1888. Nevada introduced cyanide gas in 1924 as a "more humane way" of executing criminals. Lethal injections were introduced by Oklahoma in 1977.[15]

The 1930s saw an average of 167 executions a year. There were 1289 executions in the 1940s, 715 in the 1950s, and 191 from 1960 to 1972, when the United States Supreme Court rendered its decision in *Furman v. Georgia.* [16]

In *Furman* the Supreme Court held that punishment would be deemed to be "cruel and unusual" under the Eighth Amendment to the United States Constitution, if it was too severe for the crime, if it was arbitrary or offended society's sense of justice, or if it was not more effective than a less severe penalty. Based upon this standard, the Supreme Court, by a 5 to 4 vote, found that Georgia's death penalty statute, which gave the jury unbridled sentencing discretion, could result in arbitrary sentencing rendering the punishment "cruel and usual," and in violation of the Eighth Amendment. By virtue of

---

14 Death Penalty Information Center, "History of the Death Penalty: Part I," citing L. Randa; W.Schabas, *The Abolition of the Death Penalty in International Law* (Cambridge University Press, 2nd ed., 1997); and R. Bohn, *Deathquest: An Introduction to the Theory and Practice of Capital Punishment in the United States* (Anderson Publishing, 1999). The article states that in 1794, Pennsylvania repealed the death penalty for all offenses other than "first degree murder"; and in 1946 Michigan became the first state to ban executions except for treason.

15 Ibid.

16 Ibid.; Furman v. Georgia, 408 U.S. 238 (1972).

this decision, the Supreme Court effectively voided 40 similar type death penalty statutes, resulting in the commutation of 629 death row sentences, and placing a moratorium on further executions because the statutes were no longer effective.[17]

It seems ironic that states previously enacted statutes, allowing for the discretionary application of the death penalty, in order to avoid the mandatory imposition of such punishment in cases that may not seem warranted on the facts. It was this same discretionary application that the Supreme Court found objectionable in *Furman.*

Justices Brennan and Marshall stated in *Furman* that the death penalty in itself was "cruel and unusual punishment" and therefore unconstitutional. The other justices limited their decision to the specific statutes, as written, as being unconstitutional. This allowed states to enact new statutes that ended the arbitrariness in the manner of sentencing that the Supreme Court found unconstitutional in *Furman.* Florida took the lead in that regard within five months after *Furman* was decided. Thirty-four other states followed suit, with some of those states removing all discretion and mandating capital punishment for those convicted of capital crimes. The Supreme Court, however, struck down the practice of mandatory punishment in 1976 in *Woodson v. North Carolina.* [18]

Other states enacted sentencing guidelines for the judge and jury to utilize when imposing the death sentence. These guidelines allowed for the introduction of aggravating and mitigating factors in determining the sentence to be imposed. The Supreme Court in *Gregg v. Georgia* approved these types of guidelines.[19] *Gregg* further approved other procedural reforms: bifurcated trials, where the jury would first deliberate to consider the guilt of the accused and, if found guilty, the jury would deliberate again to recommend the sentence to be

---

17 Ibid.

18 Ibid., Woodson v. North Carolina, 428 U.S. 280 (1976).

19 Gregg v. Georgia, 428 U.S. 153 (1976).

imposed; the practice of automatic appellate review of convictions and sentences; and "proportionality review," a process whereby the state appellate courts could compare the sentence in the case being reviewed with other cases within the state to determine if it is disproportionate. *Gregg* did not require that all of these procedural safeguards needed to be adopted in the new statutes under review. In the final analysis, *Gregg* held that the new death penalty statutes enacted in Florida, Georgia and Texas were constitutional, effectively reinstating and validating the death penalty in those states.[20]

Although the Supreme Court continues to uphold the right of states to enforce statutes permitting execution for capital crimes, the Court limited the application of capital punishment under certain circumstances. For example, the Court held in *Thompson v. Oklahoma* [21] that no state without a minimum age provided in its death penalty statute could execute someone who was under sixteen at the time of the commission of the crime. The Court held in *Coker v. Georgia* [22] that the death penalty is unconstitutional punishment for the rape of a woman who did not die.

In January 1977, executions again began with Gary Gilmore dying by firing squad in Utah. An additional 819 persons have been executed from then through 2002. As of January 1, 2003 there are over 3,700 prisoners on death row awaiting their executions. Thirty-eight of the 50 states have statutes that provide a death penalty for certain crimes. There are also death penalties provided by Federal statutes and the Military Code of Justice. [23]

---

20 Ibid.

21 Thompson v. Oklahoma, 487 U.S. 815 (1988).

22 Coker v. Georgia, 433 U.S. 584 (1977).

23 Amnesty International, http://web.amnesty.org/library/Index/ENGACT500072003

The nations of the world have not been in alignment with the United States with respect to the application of the death penalty. In 1948 the United Nations General Assembly adopted the Universal Declaration of Human Rights that proclaimed a universal "right to life." Subsequent human rights treaties were enacted during the 1950s and 1960s. These documents provide for the "right to life," but also permit the death penalty as an exception that must only be used under the strictest procedural safeguards. Despite this exception, 62 countries had stopped using capital punishment by 1980, either pursuant to law or by practice. By 1999 this practice had been adopted by 105 countries. Although more than half of the countries in the world have abolished the death penalty completely, *de facto*, or for ordinary crimes, over 90 countries still retain the death penalty, including the United States, Iran and China. [24]

Amnesty International reports that more than 3,248 people were sentenced to death in 67 countries, and 1,526 people were executed in 31 countries during 2002. 1,060 of these executions occurred in China, 113 in Iran, and 71 in the United States. These three countries accounted for 81 percent of the executions that occurred during 2002. [25]

By 2003, according to Amnesty International, 76 countries and territories presently had abolished the death penalty for all crimes; 15 countries had abolished the death penalty for all but exceptional crimes, such as wartime crimes; and 21 countries could be considered abolitionists in practice because they retained the death penalty

---

24 Death Penalty Information Center, "History of the Death Penalty: Part II," www.deathpenaltyinfo.org/ history3.html, citing W. Schabas, *The Abolition of the Death Penalty in International Law* (Cambridge University Press, 2nd ed., 1997); Amnesty International, List of Abolitionist and Retentionist Countries, (Report ACT 50/01/99, April 1999).

25 Amnesty International, http://web.amnesty.org/library/Index/ENGACT500072003

in law but had not carried out any executions for the past 10 years or more and were believed to have a policy or established practice of not carrying out executions. [26]

Abiding Argument for the Death Penalty

Ernest van den Haag, a proponent of the death penalty, observes that capital punishment is opposed on the grounds that it is discriminatorily or capriciously distributed among the guilty. He asserts if capital punishment is immoral in and of itself, the manner of distribution cannot affect the quality of what is distributed, whether it is punishment or reward:

> *Maldistribution of any punishment among those who deserve it is irrelevant to its justice or morality …. Guilt is personal. The only relevant question is: does the person to be executed deserve the punishment? … The ideal of equal justice demands that justice be equally distributed, not that it be replace [sic] by equality. Justice requires that as many of the guilty as possible be punished, regardless of whether others have avoided punishment.*[27]

Van den Haag recognizes that there are no conclusive statistical findings that demonstrate that the death penalty is a better deterrent than are alternative punishments. Yet, Van den Haag asserts that because of its finality, the death penalty is more feared than imprisonment and deters some potential murderers who are not deterred by the thought of imprisonment alone. Van den Haag believes that if the death penalty deters even a few potential murderers, resulting in saving the lives of their prospective victims, this is more important than

---

26 Ibid.

27 Ernest van den Haag, "The Ultimate Punishment: a Defense," http://www.pbs.org/wgbh/pages/frontline/angel/procon/haagarticle.html

preserving the lives of convicted murderers because of the probability that executing them would not deter others. [28]

Van den Haag acknowledges that punishment, regardless of motivation, is not intended to revenge a crime, to offset or compensate for the victim's suffering, or to be measured by it. Rather, the purpose of punishment is "to vindicate the law and the social order undermined by the crime." [29]

Van den Haag disagrees with the argument that by executing a murderer the state encourages, endorses, or legitimizes killing. According to Van den Haag, this argument is spurious since punishments, although meant to be unpleasant, have seldom been contended to legitimize the identical unpleasantness. By way of example, imprisonment is not thought to legitimize kidnapping, nor does the imposition of penal fines legitimize theft. Van den Haag contends that the difference between murder and a lawful execution is that the former is unlawful and undeserved, and the latter is a lawful and deserved punishment for an unlawful act. [30]

Van den Haag also argues that punishment is threatened in order to deter crime. Punishment is imposed to not only make the threats credible, but also as retribution, or justice, for those crimes that were not deterred. Legal punishment of a person found lawfully guilty cannot be unjust. "By committing the crime, the criminal volunteered to assume the risk of receiving a legal punishment that he could have avoided by not committing the crime." Furthermore, to justify the moral argument that the death penalty may be regarded as always excessive as retribution, one must believe that no crime, regardless of how heinous, could ever justify capital punishment. According to Van den Haag, such a position can neither be corroborated nor refuted, but becomes solely an article of faith. Van den

---

28 Ibid.

29 Ibid.

30 Ibid.

Haag adjudges as nonsense the belief that everybody – the murderer as well as the victim – has a natural right to life and that the law should not deprive anyone of life, including the murderer.[31]

Against the background of this review of the death penalty in society, let us now turn to a biblical and Christian inquiry. We begin with the Hebrew Scriptures, then examine the teachings of Jesus and the New Testament, followed by an examination of the classical argument by Cardinal Avery Dulles, and finally take up the new development in Catholic social teaching against the death penalty, especially as led by the late Pope John Paul II.

WHAT THE HEBREW SCRIPTURES SAY

The Book of Genesis records the murder by Cain of Abel and the punishment imposed for that crime:[32]

> *The Lord then said: "What have you done! Listen: Your brother's blood cries out to me from the soil! Therefore you shall be banned from the soil that opened its mouth to receive your brother's blood from your hand. If you till the soil, it shall no longer give you its produce. You shall become a restless wanderer on the earth." Cain said to the Lord: "My punishment is too great to bear. Since you have now banished me from the soil, and I must avoid your presence and become a restless wanderer on the earth, any one may kill me at sight." "Not so!" the Lord said to him. "If anyone kills Cain, Cain shall be avenged sevenfold." So the Lord put a mark on Cain, lest anyone should kill him at sight. Cain then left the Lord's presence and settled in the land of Nod, east of Eden.*

The punishment for murder became banishment and exile, with the murderer being marked for life for his crime but also for protection. The first mention of death as a crime for murder arises later in

31 Ibid.

32 Genesis 4:11-15.

Genesis 9:6, with God speaking to Noah and his family after the great flood:

> *Only flesh with its lifeblood still in it you shall not eat. For your own lifeblood, too, I will demand an accounting; from every animal I will demand it, and from man in regard to his fellow man I will demand an accounting for human life. If anyone sheds the blood of man, shall man shed his blood; for in the image of God has man been made.*

This passage considers that the death of a human is an offense against God because humans are made in the image of God. Whereas the previous passage involving Cain required only that the murderer be exiled, this later passage concerning Noah requires that anyone who "sheds the blood" of another human shall have his blood shed by humans. This later passage thus appears to present the first "authority" for capital punishment.

Another biblical passage requires that "murderers" be put to death, even permitting the avenger to be the executioner.[33] People who killed another unintentionally, however, were allowed to take refuge from such avengers in established places of asylum.[34]

The Hebrew Scriptures contain numerous other references that require the imposition of death as punishment for the "crime":[35]

- sacrificing to any other god;[36]
- when a stranger enters the Temple;[37]
- any person who urges an Israelite to follow other gods;[38]

---

33 Numbers 35:16-21.

34 Numbers 35:9-15; 22-28.

35 See generally "What the bible Says About the Death Penalty/Capital Punishment." http://www.religioustolerance.org/exe_bibl.htm

36 Exodus 22:19; Numbers 25:1-15.

37 Numbers 1:51; Numbers 3:10, 18:7 and 17:13.

38 Deuteronomy 13:1-11.

- a man or woman who acts as a fortune teller;[39] being a sorceress;[40]
- anyone who commits bestiality;[41]
- anyone who curses his father or mother;[42]
- anyone who commits adultery;[43]
- anyone who is not a virgin when she marries and has sexual relations with her husband, even if she claims to be a virgin;[44]
- a male who lies with another male as with a woman;[45]
- marrying a woman and her mother;[46]
- a woman who attempts to mate with an animal;[47]
- having sexual relations with a betrothed maiden;[48]
- kidnapping a fellow Israelite in order to enslave him and sell him;[49]
- being a "stubborn and unruly son who will not listen to his father and mother, and not obey them…";[50]

---

39 Leviticus 20:27.

40 Exodus 22:17.

41 Exodus 22:18; Leviticus 20:15.

42 Exodus 20:9.

43 Leviticus 20:10-12; Deuteronomy 22:22.

44 Deuteronomy 22: 13-21.

45 Leviticus 20:13.

46 Leviticus 20:14.

47 Leviticus 20:16.

48 Deuteronomy 22:23-27.

49 Deuteronomy 24:7.

- blaspheming the Lord's name;[51]
- working on the Sabbath;[52]
- being a false witness, who shall be punished to the same extent to which he accused his kinsman falsely ("Life for life, eye for eye, tooth for tooth, hand for hand, and foot for foot!);[53]
- any man who refuses to listen to the officiating priest; [54]
- when men fight and injure a pregnant women they shall receive the same punishment that they inflicted on the woman, "life for life, eye for eye, tooth for tooth, hand for hand, foot for foot, burn for burn, wound for wound, stripe for stripe";[55]
- an owner of oxen who gored someone to death. [56]

Further, under Hebrew law, an accused murderer could only be convicted on the testimony of two or three witnesses.[57]

WHAT THE NEW TESTAMENT SAYS

In the New Testament, we find that Jesus was charged and put to death under the guise of blasphemy.[58] So was Stephen, the first Christian martyr after Jesus' death.[59]

---

50 Deuteronomy 22:18.

51 Leviticus 24:16.

52 Exodus 35:2-3.

53 Deuteronomy 19:21.

54 Deuteronomy 17:12.

55 Exodus 21: 22-25.

56 Exodus 21:28-29.

57 Numbers 35:30; Deuteronomy 17:6; see Hebrews 10:28.

58 Mark 14:62.

59 Acts 6:8-7:60.

During Jesus' life, we have the story of a woman, accused of committing adultery, on the verge of being put to death by her accusers. Jesus does not appear to challenge the accusers' right under Mosaic Law to stone the woman to death. He does, however, challenge those men only to inflict that punishment if they themselves are without sin.[60]

Jesus states in other passages that it "is mercy I desire and not sacrifice."[61] In the Sermon on the Mount, Jesus instructs his disciples to seek no revenge for wrongdoing.[62] He also teaches them even to love their enemies.[63]

Despite Jesus' witness, Saint Paul's *Letter to the Romans* is customarily invoked to support the proposition that the governing state has the authority, as the "servant of God," to administer capital punishment.

> *For rulers are not a cause of fear to good conduct, but to evil. Do you wish to have no fear of authority? Then do what is good and you will receive approval from it, for it is a servant of God for your good. But if you do evil, be afraid, for it does not bear the sword without purpose; it is the servant of God to inflict wrath on the evildoer.* [64]

Cardinal Dulles' Statement of the Classical Argument

In his essay "Catholicism & Capital Punishment," Cardinal Avery Dulles points out that other passages of the New Testament also appear to support the authority of the ruling authorities to impose a death sentence. Further, he observes that divine punishment was

---

60 John 8:3-11.

61 Matthew 9:13.

62 Matthew 5:38-39.

63 Matthew 5:43-44.

64 Romans 13:3-4.

deemed warranted in the case of Ananias and Sapphira, when Peter rebuked them for their fraudulent action.[65]

He notes that the Letter to the Hebrews states: "A man who has violated the Law of Moses dies without mercy at the testimony of two or three witnesses." And "Peter admonishes Christians to be subject to emperors and governors, who have been sent by God to punish those who do wrong."[66]

Cardinal Dulles then goes on to state that "no passage in the New Testament disapproves of the death penalty," nor does Scripture report Jesus ever denying that the State had authority to exact capital punishment, even in connection with his own crucifixion or that of the two thieves who were crucified with him. [67]

In addition, Cardinal Dulles emphasizes "that the Fathers and Doctors of the Church are virtually unanimous in their support for capital punishment," even though the clergy are not to pronounce the death sentences or to serve as executioners.[68] He quotes St. Augustine, who writes in *The City of God*:

> *The same divine law which forbids the killing of a human being allows certain exceptions, as when God authorizes killing by a general law or when He gives an explicit commission to an individual for a limited time. Since the agent of authority is but a sword in the hand, and is not responsible for the killing, it is no way contrary to the commandment "Thou shall not kill" to wage war at God's bidding,*

---

65 Acts 5:1-14; see Cardinal Avery Dulles, "Catholicism & Capital Punishment," *First Things: A Journal of Religious and Public Life*, 112 (April 2001): 30-35.

66 Hebrews 10:28; 1 Peter 2:13; Cardinal Avery Dulles, "Catholicism & Capital Punishment."

67 Ibid.

68 Ibid.

or for the representative of the State's authority to put criminals to death, according to law or the rule of rational justice. [69]

Arguing that the death penalty is meant to be an exercise of judgment and not of hate, Cardinal Dulles cites the statement of Pope Innocent III:

We assert concerning the power of the state that it is able to exercise the judgment of blood, without mortal sin, provided it proceed to inflict the punishment not in hate, but in judgment; not incautiously, but after consideration.[70]

Cardinal Dulles also notes that the original Roman Catechism, issued three years after the conclusion of the Council of Trent in 1566, taught "that the power of life and death had been entrusted by God to civil authorities and that the use of this power, far from involving the crime of murder, is an act of paramount obedience to the Fifth Commandment – "Thou shall not kill."[71] He then reminds us that later authorities such as Robert Bellarmine, Alphonsus Liguori, Francisco de Vitoria, Thomas More, Francisco Suarez and John Henry Newman also recognized that certain criminals and crimes should be punished by death.[72] He points out that from 1929 to 1969 the Vatican City State had a penal code that included the death penalty for anyone who attempted to assassinate the pope.[73]

Even as late as 1992, with the issuance of the modern *Catechism of the Catholic Church,* it was recognized that:

---

69 Ibid.

70 Dwyer, Judith A. (ed.), *The New Dictionary of Catholic Thought*, "Capital Punishment," Liturgical Press (Collegeville, MN. 1994), quoting from Anti-Waldensian Profession, DS, no. 795.

71 Ibid.

72 Ibid.

73 Ibid.

> *Preserving the common good of society requires rendering the aggressor unable to inflict harm. For this reason the traditional teaching of the Church has acknowledged as well-founded the right and duty of legitimate public authority to punish malefactors by means of penalties commensurate with the gravity of the crime, not excluding, in cases of extreme gravity, the death penalty... The primary effect of punishment is to redress the disorder caused by the offense. When his punishment is voluntarily accepted by the offender, it takes on the value of expiation. Moreover, punishment has the effect of preserving public order and the safety of persons. Finally, punishment has a medicinal value; as far as possible it should contribute the correction of the offender... If bloodless means are sufficient to defend human lives against an aggressor and to protect public order and the safety of persons, public authority should limit itself to such means, because they better correspond to the concrete conditions of the common good and are more in conformity to the dignity of the human person.*[74]

Although Cardinal Dulles acknowledges that the State has the right to employ capital punishment, nevertheless he observes that the primary purposes of criminal punishment in the Catholic tradition are: rehabilitation – to seek to bring the criminal to repentance and moral reform; defense against the criminal – to protect society by preventing the criminal from committing additional crimes; deterrence – to discourage further violence or the commission of other crimes; and retribution – to restore the right order violated by the crime.[75] Under present Catholic thought, capital punishment can be applied "if this is the only possible way of effectively defending human lives against the unjust aggressor."[76]

Cardinal Dulles recognizes that although the imposition of the death sentence can move a convicted person to repentance and conver-

---

74 *Catechism of the Catholic Church* (1992) at §§2266 and 2267.

75 Cardinal Avery Dulles, "Catholicism and Capital Punishment."

76 Most. Rev. Sean O'Malley, OFM Cap., "Pastoral Letter on Capital Punishment" (February 25, 1999); see *Catechism of the Catholic Church* at §2267.

sion, it effectively precludes any possible rehabilitation and reintegration of the convicted person with society.[77] Likewise, he concedes that capital punishment is an effective way of precluding the convicted person from committing another crime in the future and thereby protecting society from him/her. However, life imprisonment in a secure facility could accomplish the same purpose.[78] Whether the execution of one criminal deters other persons from committing similar or other types of crimes is open to debate, with statistics supporting each view depending upon which side of the position you occupy.

Cardinal Dulles recognizes that "guilt calls for punishment. The graver the offense, the more severe the punishment ought to be."[79] He summarizes Thomas Aquinas' position

> *... that sin calls for deprivation of some good, such as, in serious cases, the good of temporal or even eternal life. By consenting to the punishment of death, the wrongdoer is placed in a position to expiate his evil deeds and escape punishment in the next life... even if the malefactor is not repentant, he is benefited by being prevented from committing more sins.* [80]

The concern of Cardinal Dulles, however, is whether the retributive goal of punishment becomes a self-assertive act of vengeance by the will of the governed, especially since "according to the Christian faith, God 'will render to every man according to his works' at the final judgment" and "retribution by the State can only be a symbolic anticipation of God's perfect justice."[81] Cardinal Dulles asserts, "For the symbolism to be authentic, the society must believe in the exis-

---

77 Ibid.

78 Ibid.

79 Ibid.

80 Ibid.

81 Ibid.; Romans 2:6; cf. Matthew 16:27.

tence of a transcendent order of justice, which the State has an obligation to protect."[82]

Cardinal Dulles believes that although government may have at some past point in time recognized the transcendent order of justice, which it was obligated to protect, nevertheless, in our time the government is merely viewed as an instrument of the governed. As a result, rather than capital punishment being government's recognition and attempt to protect the "transcendent order of justice," it may amount to nothing more than government submitting itself to the vengeance, collective anger, or vindictiveness of the governed. This would be "reprehensible" and morally insufficient to justify its use.[83]

A Gallup poll conducted in October 2002 revealed that 70% of Americans said they support the death penalty. 52% supported the use of the death penalty when life without parole was an option. Only 53% felt that the death penalty was applied fairly.[84] Cardinal Dulles necessarily presumes that the support of the death penalty by these "governed" is motivated by factors other than a recognition and belief that the murder of innocent victims violates a "transcendent order of justice," intended for humanity, that needs to be protected and maintained.[85] To protect and maintain this order of justice, the inherent dignity of humans, and their right to life, may re-

---

82 Cardinal Avery Dulles, "Catholicism and Capital Punishment."

83 Ibid.

84 Office of Social Development & World Peace, United States Conference of Catholic Bishops, "The Death Penalty" (February 2003).

85 Without further data, one is unable to verify whether Cardinal Dulles' assumption concerning the motives of the "governed" is valid, especially since our faith subscribes to the belief that humans are made in the image and likeness of God and, as a result, have the inherent capacity to strive to seek the "transcendent order of justice." Of course, this capacity can be blurred by other motives, as suggested by Cardinal Dulles, such as vengeance, collective anger, and vindictiveness.

quire that the temporal lives of those persons who have deliberately taken the life of an innocent victim be forfeited.

Based upon his review of Scripture and tradition, Cardinal Dulles recognizes this principle:

> *Summarizing the verdict of Scripture and tradition, we can glean some settled points of doctrine. It is agreed that crime deserves punishment in this life and not only in the next. In addition, it is agreed that the State has authority to administer appropriate punishment to those judged guilty of crimes and that this punishment may, in serious cases, include the sentence of death.*[86]

THE DEVELOPMENT IN CATHOLIC SOCIAL TEACHING

Although Scripture and tradition accepted the classical view that the death penalty was appropriate punishment for certain serious cases, the judgment is now made by the Catholic tradition that the death penalty for the most part is no longer necessary to defend the community.

Reflecting the new developments in Catholic social teaching about the death penalty, particularly as promoted by Pope John Paul II, the classical teaching reflected in the *Catechism of the Catholic Church* was modified in 1997. The sections cited above (2267 & 2266) were revised to read as follows:

> *The efforts of the state to curb the spread of behavior harmful to people's rights and to the basic rules of civil society correspond to the requirement of safeguarding the common good. Legitimate public authority has the right and the duty to inflict punishment proportionate to the gravity of the offense. Punishment has the primary aim of redressing the disorder introduced by the offense. When it is willingly accepted by the guilty party, it assumes the value of expiation. Punishment, then, in addition to defending public order and protecting*

---

86 Ibid.

people's safety, has a medicinal purpose: as far as possible, it must contribute to the correction of the guilty party.

Assuming that the guilty party's identity and responsibility have been fully determined, the traditional teaching of the Church does not exclude recourse to the death penalty, if this is the only possible way of effectively defending human lives against the unjust aggressor. If, however, non-lethal means are sufficient to defend and protect people's safety from the aggressor, the revised Catechism argues that public authority should limit itself to such means, as these are more in keeping with the concrete conditions of the common good and more in conformity with the dignity of the human person.

Today, in fact, as a consequence of the possibilities which the state has for effectively preventing crime, by rendering one who has committed an offense incapable of doing harm – and at the same time without definitively taking away from him the possibility of redeeming himself – the cases in which the execution of the offender is an absolute necessity "are very rare, if not practically non-existent."[87]

Thus Pope John Paul II recently wrote:

The new evangelization calls for followers of Christ who are unconditionally pro-life: who will proclaim, celebrate and serve the Gospel of life in every situation. A sign of hope is the increasing recognition that the dignity of human life must never be taken away, even in the case of someone who has done great evil. Modern society has the means of protecting itself, without definitively denying criminals the chance to reform. I renew the appeal I made most recently at Christmas for a consensus to end the death penalty, which is both cruel and unnecessary.[88]

---

87 *Catechism of the Catholic Church* (1997) at §§2266 and 2267, citing John Paul II, Evangelium Vitae, 56.

88 Pope John Paul II, January 27, 1999, St. Louis, Missouri (http://www.nccbuscc.org/sdwp/national/criminal/appeal.htm).

Further, at least two other issues need to be examined. First, the death penalty is irrevocable and has resulted in the execution of innocent persons. Some persons who have been executed were later determined to have been innocent of the crime. Other persons awaiting execution have been found to be innocent and were subsequently freed. Second, it has also been argued that the death penalty has been disproportionately applied to minorities.

The inability to resolve these issues with any reasonable degree of certainty has led George Ryan, the former Governor of Illinois, when leaving office in January 2003, to commute the sentences of all 167 prisoners on the state's death row.

In reflecting on Catholic teaching, Cardinal Mahoney concludes:

> *Even the most hardened criminal remains a human person, created in God's image, and possessing a dignity, value, and worth which must be recognized, promoted, safeguarded and defended. Simply put, we believe that every person is sacred, every life is precious – even the life of one who has violated the rights of others by taking a life. Human dignity is not qualified by what we do. It cannot be earned or forfeited. Human dignity is an irrevocable character of each and every person.*[89]

The death penalty cheapens the value and dignity of life. In the words of the Administrative Board of the Catholic bishops, our society's increased reliance on the death penalty

> *...diminishes all of us and is a sign of growing disrespect for human life. We cannot overcome crime by simply executing criminals, nor can we restore the lives of the innocent by ending the lives of those convicted of their murders. The death penalty offers the tragic illusion that we can defend life by taking life ... Through education, through advocacy, and through prayer and contemplation on the life of Jesus, we must commit ourselves to a persistent and principled witness against the*

89 Cardinal Roger Mahoney, "A Witness To Life: The Catholic Church and the Death Penalty" (May 25, 2000).

death penalty, against a culture of death, and for the Gospel of Life.[90]

Archbishop Sean O'Malley writes: "When human life under any circumstances is not held as sacred in a society, all human life is diminished and threatened."[91] Promoting the State's right to kill people who have killed other people only continues to feed the "cycle of violence" or "cycle of revenge" that facilitates a culture of death. According to Archbishop O'Malley, "Violence should not be our response to violence....State sponsored violence will not promote a new respect for life but only serve to erode reverence for life even more."[92]

This sentiment is echoed by Correta Scott King, widow of Dr. Martin Luther King:

> *As one whose husband and mother-in-law have died victims of murder and assassination, I stand firmly and unequivocally opposed to the death penalty for those convicted of capital offenses. An evil deed is not redeemed by an evil deed of retaliation. Justice is never advanced in the taking of a human life. Morality is never upheld by a legalized murder.*[93]

We are called to replace the culture of death with a culture of life. "But a culture of life rests on the foundational principle that all are created in God's image. We are called to uphold the life and dignity of every human being at all times including the lives of those justly convicted of horrible crimes." [94]

---

90 Administrative Board of the United States Conference of Catholic Bishops, "A Good Friday Appeal to End the Death Penalty" (April 2, 1999).

91 Most. Rev. Sean O'Malley, OFM Cap., "Pastoral Letter on Capital Punishment" (February 25, 1999).

92 Ibid.

93 Ibid.

94 Cardinal Roger Mahony and Cardinal William Keeler, "Approaching the Exe-

As stated in *Living the Gospel of Life: A Challenge to American Catholics:*

> *Our witness to respect for life shines most brightly when we demand respect for each and every human life, including the lives of those who fail to show that respect for others. The antidote to violence is love, not more violence.*[95]

My heart pains when I read that someone has been brutally murdered, especially when it is a young innocent child. My initial reaction is one of despair, questioning what could possibly cause one human to want deliberately and brutally to take the life of another human. Can we ever hope to stop murder? More importantly, can we ever hope to stop murder with more "legalized" killing? I think not. My hope is only that if we continue to choose life, even when others do not, we are heading along the right path that eventually leads to ultimate life, justice, and peace.

---

cution of Timothy McVeigh" (May 2, 2001).

95 United States Conference of Catholic Bishops, *Living the Gospel of Life: A Challenge to American Catholics* (December 3, 1998), 22.

6

THE DEATH PENALTY IN THE HISTORY OF CHRISTENDOM

JAMES J. MEGIVERN, PH.D.
Professor of Religion Emeritus
University of North Carolina Wilmington

Dr. Megivern is the author of the fullest and now standard work on capital punishment in Christian history. His essay here is an expanded version of a lecture delivered at the annual meeting of the American Philosophical Society, Benjamin Franklin Hall, Philadelphia, PA, April 26, 2002.
It offers an important summary of his text.

The death penalty and war have long been linked as practices that present special problems for any professedly Christian ethic. What they have most obviously in common is that both engage directly in the intentional destruction of human life. The fact that they were already standard practices in both Roman and Jewish cultures in which Christianity first arose accounts in large part for their eventual acceptance, especially since the Hebrew law codes with some three dozen capital statutes were part of the scriptures inherited as the Christian Old Testament. But this does not mean that there were no questions or struggles over their gaining the mantle of legitimacy.

Part of the problem which has been all too little explored was that it was not the Hebrew Scriptures with the framework of Rabbinical interpretation that were inherited but their Greek translation, the Septuagint, which was adopted as prologue to the New Testament writings to form the Christian Bible. This meant that they came to be viewed in an entirely different context in the Greco-Roman culture. One feature that was lost was the restraint in the actual use of death as a penalty in the ancient Hebrew ethos.[1]

Uneasiness over the ready recourse to lethal violence in Roman Law led to serious reservations about any *Christian* involvement, even while conceding to the pagan state the legal right to take life (so, e.g., Origen).[2] Later developments conspired to erode this broad negativity toward killing, without openly abandoning the principle that "the Church abhors bloodshed."

After all, every execution in the New Testament is seen as an unjust abuse of authority: the beheading of John the Baptist, the crucifixion of Jesus, the stoning of Stephen, not to mention the traditions of the martyrdoms of Peter and Paul and so many others under Emperor Nero, all the way down to Emperor Diocletian. The very notion of "witnessing" with one's blood (martyrdom) is but the flip side of unjust state-authorized death penalties. Early Christians had ample opportunity to see the concrete reality of capital punishment as all too often the tool of raw power politics.

---

1 See Edna Erez, "Thou Shalt Not Execute: Hebrew Law Perspective on Capital Punishment," *Criminology* 19:1 (May 1981). Also, Gardner C. Hanks, *Capital Punishment and the Bible* (Scottsdale, PA: Herald Press, 2002), especially chapter 2, "The Mosaic Law."

2 Origen, Against Celsus 7:26. See Lisa Sowle Cahill, *Love Your Enemies: Discipleship, Pacifism, and Just War Theory* (Minneapolis, MN: Fortress Press, 1994), 53.

With the fourth century conversion of Constantine and the adoption of Christianity as the preferred religion of the Roman Empire, however, Christians found themselves cast – willy-nilly – in the role of potential executioners. The problems this created were monumental and the stances adopted were diverse. The case of Priscillian, heretical Bishop of Avila, in 385 was the first documented instance of Christians condemning fellow Christians to death for doctrinal differences. Most significantly, however, this act provoked outrage from the most respected church leaders of the day. Bishops Martin of Tours, Ambrose of Milan, and Sergius of Rome all protested vehemently and severed communion with the bishops who had approved.[3] It was an ominous event that cast a long shadow down the centuries. The Theodosian Code of a half-century later further manifested that Roman Law in Christian hands was not to be marked by any special leniency but actually at times entailed greater harshness than in its pre-Christian form.

It is thus beyond question that ambivalence characterized the status of the death penalty throughout the early centuries of the Christian state-church experience. The right of the civil authorities to use it against those who were serious threats to the social order was not generally disputed, but its use against religious dissidents was problematic in the extreme. Two different contentions collided here and the issue was left unresolved. No one illustrates this ambivalence more agonizingly than St. Augustine, who saw the state as having the theoretical right to execute, but who invariably called for it not to be used in actual practice.[4]

---

3 See Henry Chadwick, *Priscillian of Avila* (Oxford: Clarendon Press, 1976), especially chapter 3, "Priscillian's End and its Consequences."

4 See Nice to Fernández Blázquez, O.P., *La Pena de Muerte según San Agustín* (Madrid: Ediciones Augustinus Revista, 1975).

It is at this point that questions must be raised about the adequacy of later historiography. There is clearly a "missing story" that has to be reconstructed if any sense is to be made of how capital punishment came to be uncritically entrenched in subsequent Christian practice. The critical scholarship needed to achieve this is, for a number of reasons, only in its early stages. My own work is little more than an initial survey, suggesting some of the areas that call for far greater attention and sharper analysis. The following series of ten theses is an attempt to abbreviate and summarize the state of the question.

1. *The Problem of Heresy.* The positive acceptance of the death penalty in the Christian Church has its roots in the intractable problem of heresy. Once the church was in the position of being the state religion, inseparably united with the empire, the use of political power to enforce correct doctrine created a situation which virtually guaranteed compromise of earlier ethical ideals. It was the Emperor who called the Councils (starting with Nicaea in 325) and pressed the bishops to formulate both doctrine and practice in such ways as to promote imperial unity. This is where the real problem starts, and it is where Saints Ambrose and Augustine worked desperately to come up with an ethic that would allow legitimate use of violence ("agonized participation"), fenced in with strict conditions and limitations so as to prevent it from turning into a policy of raw bloodshed.

2. *The Question of Intention.* One result of this fourth-century dilemma, grappled with by the best Christian minds of the age, was a legacy of ambivalence, which took various detours over the next seven centuries. The valiant Augustinian effort to limit violence by restricting it to the absolute minimum necessary as a last resort, while insisting that one could never allow it to turn into revenge, created its own problems, not the least of which was its challenging psychology. How was one to manage, in the very act of destroying the life of another, to maintain the intention of love for one's enemy as Jesus had

commanded?[5] Even the attempt to believe that one was doing so seemed an open invitation to engage in some kind of hypocrisy.

Historians examining these centuries have regularly passed on with little comment other than the assurance that there was already universal consensus on the legitimacy of the death penalty. More critical investigation and evaluation is surely warranted. Isolated statements of leaders that raise questions about the validity of such a simple stance need to be confronted more seriously.

For instance, Pope Gregory I at the end of the sixth century, when his integrity was questioned because of the mysterious death of a bishop imprisoned in Rome, answered his critics with the straightforward assertion that "Since I fear God, I shrink from having anything whatsoever to do with the death of anyone."[6] And in mid-ninth century Pope Nicholas I, writing to the newly converted Bulgars, actually urged them to do away with the death penalty: "You must give up your former habits and not merely avoid every occasion of taking life, but also… save the life of body and soul of each individual… not only the innocent but also criminals, because Christ has saved you from the death of the soul."[7] It is not going beyond the data to say that such incidents at least show that there continued to be a significant measure of ambivalence about Christian involvement in killing into the eleventh century.

3. *The Papal Monarchy.* It is also amply evident that an extraordinary change took place in the eleventh century, with the emergence of the "Papal Monarchy" as a result of the Gregorian Reform.[8] It was espe-

---

5 The bewildering effort could still be seen after the battle of Hastings (1066), when the victorious troops of William the Conqueror, while flying the Papal banner, lined up before their bishops to receive penances for every death they had caused on the battlefield.

6 Gregory I, *Letter to Sabinianus, Liber IV, epistula 47* (Patrologia Latina 77:721).

7 Nicholas I, *Epistula 97*, cap. 25 (866).

8 See Colin Morris, The Papal Monarchy: the Western Church from 1050 to 1250 (Oxford: Clarendon Press, 1989).

cially in the practical order that an entirely new situation arose due to the unprecedented sacralization of the sword and the consequent creation of "Christian knights."[9] The ethical novelty of this development has not received the attention it deserves. It not only legitimated but also consecrated the use of lethal violence as long as it was directed toward the "good of the church." This led very quickly to the next novelty, the invention of the "Crusade."

4. *The Crusades.* Pope Urban II called in 1095 for a new kind of work of Christian piety, enlistment in a "Crusade," which would not only allow direct killing of non-Christians ("infidels"), but in the process such conduct was reevaluated as positively virtuous, removing restraints and granting plenary indulgences rather than imposing ambivalent Augustinian penances (as had still been the practice thirty years earlier at Hastings). Once more, it is only in recent years that the magnitude of change involved in the invention of the Crusade has been confronted.[10] The "moral triumphalism" that marked earlier Christian treatments of the Crusades is an example of the same uncritical approach found in dealing with the history of the use of the death penalty.

5. *Impact on Canon Law.* Although these eleventh-century developments represented a monumental change in Christian ethics, it was the twelfth century that had to grapple with the intellectual challenge providing justification for it. The tension is palpable in the famous Causa 23 of Gratian's *Decretum* (c. 1140).[11] He struggles with the

---

9 See, e.g., *Arnold Benjamin, German Knighthood, 1050-1300* (Oxford: Clarendon Press, 1985).

10 See, for example, Jonathan Riley-Smith, *The First Crusade and the Idea of Crusading* (Philadelphia, PA: University of Pennsylvania Press, 1986), and L. S. Cahill, op. cit., 48.

11 *Decretum Magistri Gratiani.* Ed. by J.-P. Migne (Paris, 1855), pars I, czusa xxiii, quaestio v (cols. 1213-1238). See the dissertation of Sally Anne Scully, *Killing ex officio: the Teachings of 12th and 13th century Canon Lawyers on the Right to Kill* (Unpublished [microfilmed] Harvard University doctoral dissertation, 1975).

anomaly of "*ex officio* Christian killing," pondering several times the troublesome words of Jesus about turning the other cheek and not taking revenge. But in the end he could only appeal to an Augustinian distinction claiming that these hard sayings of Jesus only apply to the "preparation of the heart, not the conduct of the body." This artificial disconnect between internal dispositions and external actions obviously cried out for some kind of resolution, but meantime church leaders ominously forged ahead of the theorists, incorporating into canon law a whole series of ever harsher policies in a span of less than seventy years (1184-1252).[12] Earlier ambivalence was thus swept aside and recourse to the death penalty became an entrenched legal practice, so much a part of the cultural woodwork that it was safely shielded from objection. Even petty larceny ranked as a capital crime with little objection from churchmen.[13]

6. *A Settled Question by Aquinas' Time.* It is this phenomenon of having been elevated to a special place, a "privileged pedestal" sheltering it from serious criticism that constitutes the most unusual aspect of the use of capital punishment in subsequent Christendom. It is more than a little ironic that all of this transpired and was put firmly into place in the period right before Thomas Aquinas came on the theological scene. He had perceptive insights to contribute in his treatment of the death penalty, as in so many other areas of Christian doctrine and ethics, but by his day the basic case was closed. The practice had been accepted and codified. He was, in that sense, too

---

12 1184 – Pope Lucius III issues *Ad Abolendam* ("the founding charter of the Inquisition"); 1215 – Canon III of Lateran Council IV, endorses "due punishment" for heretics to be done by the 'secular arm'; 1231 – Pope Gregory IX, in *Excommunicamus*, specifies the due punishment as burning at the stake; 1252 – Pope Innocent IV, *Ad Extirpanda* ("the most terrible of all Bulls in the history of the Inquisition") prescribed the extirpation of heresy as the chief duty of the state, and officially approved the introduction of the use of torture as one more tool for ferreting out secret heretics.

13 See R.I. Moore, *The Formation of a Persecuting Society: Power and Deviance in Western Europe 950 to 1250* (Oxford: Blackwell, 1987).

late. Objections after 1215 or so were likely to be seen as enemy attacks redolent of heresy. It was no longer an "open question" as it had been for the previous generation of theologians, like Peter the Chanter and Alan of Lille.[14] Pope and Emperor after 1231 were in perfect accord. Capital punishment had achieved the status of "traditional" policy in European Christendom, justified as being warranted by "natural law" which in turn was but reflecting divine law.[15] The defense of the basic principle seemed to distract attention from any need to set limits or establish conditions of use.

7. *The Protestant Reformation.* It is thus important to see both what did and what did not happen to the protected position of the death penalty in the 16th century. Briefly put, there were indeed fringe groups who began to raise questions and protest the prevailing Christian recourse to war and capital punishment.[16] But the major Protestant Reformers, despite all their disagreements with Rome, were at one in keeping the death penalty firmly in place on its privileged pedestal. John Calvin's execution of Michael Servetus in Geneva in 1553 is only one of the more notorious instances of continuing the "traditional" resort to capital punishment as the standard mode of both Protestant and Catholic Christians in responding to doctrinal dissent from the thirteenth century on.

---

14 See Niceto Fernández Blázquez, O.P., "La pena de muerte: Lectura critica del pensamiento de Santo Tomás," *Studia Moralia 23* (1985): 107-128. Also, Brian Calvert, "Aquinas and the Death Penalty," *The American Journal of Jurisprudence 37* (1992), 259-281. As for Peter, see John W. Baldwin, Masters, *Princes and Merchants: the Social Views of Peter the Chanter and his Circle* (Princeton University Press, 1970, pp. 318-323).

15 For the crucial role played by the canonists' importing of the principle of counterforce ("vim vi repelleret"), see the treatment of Johannes Teutonicus in Scully, pp. 306-310.

16 See, e.g., Peter Brock, *Studies in Peace History* (York: Wm. Sessions, Ltd., 1991) Also, M.E. Miller & B.N. Gingerich, eds., *The Church's Peace Witness* (Grand Rapids, MI: Wm. B. Eerdmans, 1994).

8. *The Counter-Reformation.* The Catholic Counter-Reformation did not only modify but actually further entrenched the uncritical use of the death penalty. This is evident in both theory and practice. The theoretical reinforcement can be best seen in the Roman Catechism of 1566.[17] While it is in many ways an impressive pastoral handbook full of valuable insights regarding Christian faith, it perpetuates the anomaly of the privileged pedestal. In treating the Commandment "Thou Shalt Not Kill," it does not even attempt to justify the seeming conflict but immediately declares the death penalty an "exception" to that command. In doing so it offers no explanation, no limitation, no conditions for its use. It is simply set aside at the start as an exception that needs no further treatment or defense by those engaged in instructing the faithful.

The practical reinforcement at this time, however, is even worse than the theoretical. The lowest point in the entire history of this issue occurred in 1585, in response to an admittedly vexing social problem. Brigandage in the Roman countryside was so rampant that the aging Pope Gregory XIII could not control it. So, at the conclave, which assembled upon Gregory's death, one candidate promised that, if elected, he would "fix" the problem. As Pope Sixtus V, he set about to keep his promise and in the first five months of his pontificate, he had over 7,000 Roman bandits executed and had many of their heads placed on the lampposts of the Ponte Sant'Angelo. When questioned about the propriety of his "solution" in his role as Vicar of Christ, he affirmed that he was ready to have twenty thousand executed, if that is what it would take to restore order, and thereupon had a victory medal struck to mark the occasion. Its celebratory motto reads: "Securitas Perfecta," a designation found on the gates

---

17 For a modern English translation, see *The Catechism of the Council of Trent for Parish Priests*, ed. by J.A. McHugh, O.P. and C.J. Callan, O.P. (New York: Joseph F. Wagner, 1934, p. 420).

of many graveyards.[18] The history books have passed over this with little or no comment, as if it raised no ethical questions.

9. *Enlightenment Abolitionism.* When the first abolitionist movement began, finally reflecting at least a degree of dismay with the uncritical entrenchment of capital punishment, it was inspired by the eighteenth century Enlightenment. The works of Cesare Beccaria (1764) and Voltaire (1766) persuaded many, but this promise of change was cut short by two factors: 1) as personified in the tragic figure of Robespierre, the proposed abolition of the death penalty was itself a victim of the excesses of the French Revolution; and 2) in a truly ironic development at almost the same time, the scaffold found its staunchest support in the harsh retributivism of Immanuel Kant (1797), so much so that (to maintain the metaphor) the privileged pedestal received concrete undergirding that would guarantee it a solid place until the eve of the international human rights movement in the aftermath of World War II.

It would be unfortunate, however, not to pay tribute to two American pioneers who stood firmly against state killings. The first was Philadelphia's own Dr. Benjamin Rush (1787), who showed himself to be far ahead of and superior to his time in combining religious and philosophical arguments calling for capital punishment to be eliminated from the law codes of the promising new country. He knew his contemporaries well enough to realize that they were not yet ready to abolish "the absurd and un-Christian practice," but with characteristic optimism about the future of the nation he was helping to launch, he "consecrated this humble tribute to the unborn generations of the next century," confident that they would be wiser than his own generation.[19]

---

18 See Baron Joseph A. de Hübner, *The Life and Times of Sixtus the Fifth* (London: Longmans, Green & Co., 1872), 2 vols. The title of the original German is *Der eiserne Papst* (The Iron Pope), 1932 Berlin reprint.

19 See Philip E. Mackey, *Voices Against Death: American Opposition to Capital Punishment 1787-1975* (New York: Burt Franklin & Co., 1976). Dr. Rush' position

That next century, however, had a horrendous complication that would demand unimaginable bloodshed before it could be ended. Human slavery was the "twin evil" that had also been put on its own privileged pedestal, reinforced by many churchmen who ferociously resisted its abolition. Thus, the lonely figure that clearly saw this connection long before others and found the language to describe it was Frederick Douglass.

Chairing a meeting to protest an execution in Rochester, New York, in 1858, Douglass delivered a remarkable address called "Capital Punishment is a Mockery of Justice." He pointed out that it was "an act of cold-blooded enormity, as cowardly as it is cruel ... It undermines respect for human life" and is itself the same as "the crime which it would extinguish ... a form of revenge [that is] wrong in principle and pernicious in practice; it arises out of the lowest propensities of human nature, and is opposed to the highest civilization; it has no sanction in the spirit and teachings of Christ, which everywhere abound in loving kindness and forgiveness."[20] The first of the twin evils was eliminated in the following decade, but the other is still awaiting abolition.

10. *The Human Rights Revolution.* The unparalleled destruction of human life in the excesses of World War II (from the Nazi Holocaust to obliteration bombings to atomic incinerations) created a desperation that sparked the rise of the international human rights revolution, resulting first in the United Nations Charter (1945) and then in the Universal Declaration of Human Rights (UDHR, 1948). Never before had such a vision of faith in "the dignity and worth of the human person, in equal rights of men and women of nations large and small" been so overwhelmingly expressed and endorsed by so many.[21]

---

is set forth on pp. 3 to 13.

20 See John W. Blassingame, ed., *The Frederick Douglass Papers* (New Haven, CT: Yale University Press, 1979. vol. 3:242-248).

21 Paul Gordon Lauren, *The Evolution of International Human Rights: Visions Seen*

The Recent Development in Catholic Teaching

One of the persons consulted by French jurist René Cassin in drafting the text of the UDHR was the papal nuncio to Paris, Angelo Roncalli. Ten years later he was elected Pope John XXIII and called the renewal Council, Vatican II. Then, the year he died (1963) he wrote his encyclical *Peace on Earth*, incorporating the very language of the UDHR into contemporary Catholic teaching.[22]

The full implications of this as applied to the specific issue of the death penalty took another quarter-century to work themselves out, but progressively, in the statements of the French bishops (1978), the U.S. bishops (1980), the new Catholic Catechism (1992)[23] and even more emphatically in the 1995 encyclical of Pope John Paul II *The Gospel of Life*,[24] the privileged status of the death penalty was aban-

---

(Philadelphia, PA: University of Pennsylvania Press, 1998), p. 194. The formulation in the UN Charter was further sharpened in the *Preamble of the UDHR*, which notes "recognition of the inherent dignity and of the equal and inalienable rights of all members of the human family is the foundation of freedom, justice and peace in the world."

22 Pope John XXIII, *Pacem in Terris*, paragraphs 9-10: "Any human society... must lay down as a foundation this principle: every human being is a person... By virtue of this he has right and duties of his own... which are universal, inviolable, and inalienable." Peter Riga, *Peace on Earth: A Commentary on Pope John's Encyclical* (New York: Herder & Herder, 1964), p. 74, observes that "Such a forceful elucidation of the infinite worth of the human person and of his sacred rights cannot be found in any previous papal document."

23 English translation - *Catechism of the Catholic Church.* (Rome: Urbi et Orbi Communications, 1994), paragraph 2267: "If bloodless means are sufficient to defend human lives against an aggressor and to protect public order and the safety of persons, public authority should limit itself to such means, because... they are more in conformity with the dignity of the human person."

24 Pope John Paul II, *Evangelium Vitae*. For more details of both the Catechism and the encyclical, see James J. Megivern, *The Death Penalty: A Historical and Theological Survey* (New York: Paulist Press, 1997), 426-446.

doned. If there were any grounds for uncertainty about the meaning of these texts, the ceaseless campaign of the present pope, intervening time after time to try to stop executions whenever and wherever possible, speaks far more loudly than the efforts of some conservative Catholics to make the case that little or nothing has changed.[25]

Modern critical historiography has only just begun to address the problem of the moral triumphalism that marked most of the church histories of the past four centuries, both Protestant and Catholic. One of the first to attempt the task of overcoming the moral triumphalism and directly dismantling the privileged pedestal was the French theologian Jean-Marie Aubert in his seminal work, *Christians and the Death Penalty* (1978). He saw the dire need for moving the spotlight away from the theoretical question of the state's right to execute, and focusing it instead on the practice itself, as it is actually done. He realized that "at the level of historical analysis we can only conclude that capital punishment is an evil, barbaric institution unworthy of any and every society today."[26]

Aubert published his work the very year that Pope John Paul II was elected and began his campaign to change minds and hearts and policies, to see that the deliberate killing of human beings, no matter what they have done, is incompatible with Christian personalism and should be seen as irresponsible destruction of divine handiwork which ought to be forbidden in any nation truly committed to the recognition of human dignity and the promotion of human rights.[27]

---

25 See e.g., Antonin Scalia, "God's Justice and Ours," *First Things*, #123 (May 2002), 17-21. Also Avery Cardinal Dulles, "Catholicism and the Death Penalty," *First Things*, #113 (April-May 2001), 30-35, and two issues later, "Avery Cardinal Dulles and His Critics: An Exchange on Capital Punishment," *First Things*, #115 (August-September 2001), 7-16.

26 Jean-Marie Aubert, *Chrétiens et Peine de Mort* (Paris: Desclée, 1978), 90f.

27 See *Religious Human Rights in Global Perspective: Religious Perspectives*, ed. by John Witte, Jr. and Johan D. van der Vyver (The Hague / Boston / London: Martinus Nijhoff Publishers, 1996).

7

A THEOLOGICAL REFLECTION ON THE DEATH PENALTY

SIXTO GARCIA, PH.D.
Professor of Systematic Theology
Saint Vincent de Paul Regional Seminary, Boynton Beach, Florida

Because of the importance of Dr. Megivern's major work on the history of the Christian interpretation of the death penalty, Dr. Garcia offers an essay reflecting on and summarizing Dr. Megivern's book.

The public teaching that Pope John Paul II and most national or regional episcopal conferences in the Catholic Church have addressed in recent years to the Catholic world calling for the abolition of the death penalty has issued in an era of intense controversies and debates among present-day Catholics. The debate focuses on the problem of a consistent ethic of life, not unlike the issues of abortion and economic social justice. A question being asked today is: "How can a Catholic who opposes abortion advocate, at the same time, the execution of convicted criminals?" This is related, in some fashion, to the question: "How can a Catholic who opposes abortion be indifferent and silent to situations of hunger, homelessness, racial discrimination, and related social evils?"

In this essay I intend to offer a theological reflection on the question of the death penalty. I will query the Scriptures and the Tradition of the Church to examine the unfolding of the death penalty concerns within the Church and the political milieu she has dwelt within in her historical journey. My main source of reference will be James J. Megivern's book *The Death Penalty: An Historical and Theological Survey*.[1] I will focus on Megivern's historical analysis as a springboard for further theological inquiries into the Catholic view towards the death penalty.

For the sake of method, I divide the historical development of the death penalty issue into four parts. These parts do not correspond to the exact structure of Megivern's book, but are suggested by his historical analysis.

FROM BIBLICAL TIMES TO THE EVE OF THE CONSTANTINIAN PEACE

The witness of the Hebrew Scriptures is, at best, ambiguous. The texts of Genesis 9:6 are an example: the alleged command to retributive blood shedding may simply be, as Megivern interprets it in light of his sources, of a parabolic or hortatory kind, rather than an accepted legal procedure.

Scholars have found thirty-six capital offenses in the Hebrew Scriptures[2], but again, to what extent the legislators consigned them to writing as a way of emphasizing the sacredness of the Law, or as judicial deterrents, is difficult to say, not to mention the difficulty in ascertaining how often such capital sentences were carried out.

Paul's seeming endorsement of the power to take human lives in Romans 13: 4 might be best interpreted as an acknowledgement of the right to wield arms claimed by imperial forces (what scholars refer to as the *ius gladii*, the right to the use of the sword).

Here the scholar must also take into account the unfolding of moral sensitivity that took place in the history of the people of Israel. Abraham's attempt to dole out his wife to the Pharaoh to save his life (Gen. 12: 10-20) is a reflection of a still emerging and distant awareness of God's ethical demands, especially in those specific

---

1 New York: Paulist Press, 1997.

2 Ibid, 10.

points affecting human life and dignity. Thus the acceptance and decrees of the death penalty in the history of the chosen people, at a time when Jesus' demands for forgiveness and letting-go had not been heard, need not be taken as binding at any level. The misunderstanding of this principle would provide death penalty advocates within and without the Church with an illegitimate foundation for their bloodlust.[3]

The pre-Constantinian Christian Tradition reflects a marked ambiguity. The Christian apologists Athenagoras (fl. 176) and Minucius Felix (same period), as well as the Christian lawyer/theologian Tertullian (d. ca. 235), find the shedding of blood incompatible with the acceptance of the Gospel. Other Christian writers are more ambiguous.

Thus Clement of Alexandria (d. 214) and Origen of Alexandria find no difficulty in reconciling Luke 6: 27-28 ("Love your enemies, do good to those who hate you, bless those who curse you, pray for those who injure you"[4]) with an approval of bloodletting under certain circumstances, though for Origen the Christian cannot enroll in the Roman army, since Christians are called not to shed blood. Pagans will wield arms on their behalf when there is a need to wage war and kill to defend order and peace.

The most important moment in the unfolding of the death penalty problem comes from Augustine of Hippo (354-430). In a sermon preached at Lent in 408, Augustine argues for the need to save the sinner not by killing him, but rather by affording him the opportunity for correction. In letters 133 and 134, written to two Christian magistrates presiding over the fate of two Donatist murderers, Augustine reminds them of the superiority of the Christian law of forgiveness over that of retribution. Yet Augustine does not hesitate

---

3 The problem of fundamentalist readings of the Scriptures has been treated extensively in recent literature. Cf. Raymond Brown's, *101 Questions on the Bible* (New York: Paulist Press, 1990); and his *Introduction to New Testament Christology* (New York: Paulist Press, 1995).

4 My translation from the Nestle-Aland Greek text.

to invoke the aid of Roman arms to help fight the tide of Donatism that has perverted the people in his own town. He feels the situation justifies force. Yet, even this contradiction in Augustine's praxis does not efface the depth of his intuitions against the validity of capital punishment concerning heretics. His example will be ill heeded in following centuries.

From the Constantinian Peace to the Dawn of the Modern European Enlightenment

In 313 the Roman Emperor of the West, Constantine, confirmed an agreement signed by the Roman Emperor of the East, Licinius, granting tolerance to the Christian churches as well as to other religions in the Empire. The agreement was signed in the imperial city of Milan, and from then on this decree on religious policies, known as the Edict of Milan, became the law of the land in the Empire. It would also signal the dawn of a new (and often tragic) age in the relations between church and state.

Constantine's intent to manage the affairs of the church and to make the church his private chaplaincy were ill-disguised. He brought the might of the cruel and intolerant Roman legal system to bear on real or potential threats. For the first time a secular ruler would wield the power of life or death on the enemies of both church and state.

This is reflected in the Constantinian ban on the possession and distribution of Porphyry's work *Against the Christians*. Porphyry was an outspoken anti-Christian pagan philosopher, the disciple of the great and gentle neo-Platonist Plotinus. Constantine made the violation of this ban a capital offense, an ironic if tragic decision – given the often-bloody persecution that the Christian churches had experienced at the hand of some of the previous emperors.

The later development of Christian acceptance of the death penalty is intimately predicated on two medieval phenomena: first, the developments of heresies and the Church's inability to deal with them except by force; and second, the canonization of the "holy war" concept, the pre-eminent examples of which are the Crusades.

The early medieval heresies sprang out of a prevailing popular dissatisfaction with the laxity and corruption of the clergy. Thus the followers of Leuthard (ca.1000), who claimed direct inspiration from God and led his own into a life of simplicity and poverty, were brought to court in Champagne. They were eventually reconciled, but the charismatic group of Orleans, who claimed direct motions from the Holy Spirit, was more cruelly treated. The burning of thirteen members of this group at the stake, in Orleans in 1022, constituted the first case on record of accused heretics being burned at the stake. The disciples of Gundolfo, the leader of a group of NeoDonatists who claimed that sacraments administered by sinful and unworthy clerics were invalid, were spared a similar fate when Gundolfo recanted.

But the pattern was set: these early medieval "heresies" challenged the hedonism and fiscal corruption prevalent among medieval clergy with a call to return to evangelical simplicity, and were cruelly persecuted and in many cases killed by burning at the stake. Only the voice of Bishop Wazo of Liege (1048) sounded a note of sanity in this rapidly emerging wave of bloody repression.

The canonization (romanticization) of fighting lent weight to the argument that heretics, common criminals, and above all infidels, could and indeed should be put to the sword. The preaching of the First Crusade by Urban II at Clermont in 1095, and the concept of a "Christian militia" advocated by Gregory VII (1073-1085) and Bernard of Clairvaux (1096-1153) gave impetus to the perceived view that the Church and the secular princes possessed the *ius gladii*, that is, the right to execute those who dissented with church and state in matters of doctrine, spirituality and temporal rule.

The emergence of the Waldensian movement, led by Peter Waldes, a French merchant (fl. 1170) provided further impetus for the church's and state's ever-increasing repression against heretics. The principle advocated by early Christian writers, like Origen and Ambrose of Milan (330-397), that clerics ought never to incur in bloodshed (since this would be an irregularity constituting an impediment to orders), but should rather hand the heretic over (after ascertaining the heresy) to the secular arm for punishment, finds definitive acceptance in the medieval church.

The outstanding theologian of the medieval period was Thomas Aquinas (1224/5-1274), the "Doctor Communis" and "Doctor Angelicus." Theologians grounded in any of the several Thomistic schools of theological thought (e.g., Baroque Scholasticism, Nineteenth-Century Neo-Scholasticism, Transcendental Thomism) acknowledged the difficulty of reconciling Thomas' revolutionary and compassionate theological anthropology with his harsh acceptance of the death penalty.

In assessing his view on punishment and legally executed death, the text of his *Summa Contra Gentiles*, chapter 146, comes to mind. There Thomas invoked the seemingly merciless analogy of the sick member of a human body. A surgeon will not hesitate to amputate a diseased member to save bodily life.

The flaws of the analogy are obvious. To begin with, it is not an analogy in Thomas' own sense of the word. It is a metaphor, and a deficient one at that. The relation of a given person to the whole of the polis bears no correlation with that of a member to the rest of the body. An individual person is a unique and unrepeatable reality, bearing the image and likeness of God, and claiming rights as such that no political or ecclesiastical decree can deny by juridical or canonical "amputation."

Thomas' metaphor of the sick member may perhaps be seen in a better light against other more balanced texts on punishment. In the *Summa Theologiae,* 1-2 q.87 a. 1, he argued that the sinner incurs a three-fold punishment, corresponding to the three-fold order he has breached: one, punishment inflicted by himself, viz., the guilty conscience; two, punishment from a human, that is, the legal and ecclesiastical structures; and three, punishment inflicted by God. Thus, punishment for Thomas was not a univocal reality, but rather a complex one touching on different aspects of the human person.

A more enlightening text of Thomas (*Summa Theologiae*, 2-2, q.68 a.1) says, "In life there is no punishment for punishment's sake." Thomas thus seemed to drift apart from the notion of vindictive or retributive punishment. During our historical journey, he argued, there is always a time for conversion. Only at the consummation of history will God assign definitive penalties to sinners.

Megivern muses that if Thomas had not been burdened with the political and social tradition of revenge and punishment that his century had inherited from previous ages of canonized bloodshed, he might have argued against the death penalty, given the fact that he, as any true genius synthesizer would do, provides the categories of criticism for his own uncritical and one-sided views, such as his simple and nuance-empty advocacy of the power to kill.

Yet Megivern's treatment does not address what in my opinion are the crucial theological-anthropological texts in Thomas that indirectly provide a criticism of his capital punishment views. These now follow in their original Latin, with my translation appended.

1. *"In omnia cognoscentia cognoscunt implicite Deum in quolibet cognit."* (In every act of knowledge, the (knowing) subject knows God implicitly in whatever is known): *De Veritate* q. 22. a. 2 ad. 1.

2. *"Naturaliter anima est capax gratiae."* (Of its own nature [naturally] the human spirit is capable of [attaining] grace.)

3. *"Impossible est naturalem desiderium esse inane."* (It is impossible that natural desire be frustrated.)

4. *"Gratia non-tollat naturam, sed perficiat (eam)."* (Grace does not destroy grace, but rather perfects it.)

5. *"Fides praesupponit cognitionem naturalem, sicut gratia naturam."* (Faith presupposes natural knowledge [reason], just as grace presupposes nature.)

Sections 1, 2, and 3 above reflect Thomas' dynamics of human knowledge, an open-ended epistemological process open to the Absolute; that is, in Karl Rahner's terms, a metaphysical epistemology. In every categorical act of knowing and loving, the dynamics of the finite human intellect and will affirm the reality of God. This is an existential category, that is, a human-defining category. We ARE a living hunger and craving for God.

Sections 4 and 5 above convey Thomas' theory of the relation of grace and nature. Thomas saw "nature" (creation) as the playground of grace. Nature is perfectible, that is, it has in itself an open-endedness toward God that defines its very reality. Thomas' view sharply contrasted with Augustine's pessimistic view, whereby either grace overwhelms nature, or nature is self-sufficient and dispenses with grace. For Thomas, in a manner of speaking, the more faith and the more reason, the more grace, the more "nature." Humanity is plenified by God's gracious love, which accords humanity its full human constitution. Paraphrasing Thomas, nature is more perfectly "natural" only when plenified by grace; humanity is more perfectly human only when filled with, and grounded in, God's overflowing being of love.

Thus Thomas' foundational theological anthropology contradicted his stance on the death penalty. Thomas saw the human being as possessed of such a unique, inviolable dignity on account of his/her *identity* as an open ended dynamism toward God, as being called by God, from the beginning, to the unique, life-giving finality of agapic contemplation. Karl Rahner qualified Thomas' epistemology as "knowledge (which is) the luminous radiance of love." I will return to Thomas Aquinas later.

In the later Middle Ages, William of Ockham's Nominalist philosophy (a new teaching which saw God's will as completely arbitrary) disdained the necessary relations expressed by Thomas' principle of analogy and accorded creation and humanity an uncertain, pessimistic journey over the quicksands of God's capriciousness, and so did much to undermine Thomistic optimism about the intrinsic goodness of nature, open to God's plenifying grace. Thomas' approach to humanity and creation through Plato's theory of participation in absolute being, affirmed by Thomas through his sense of the analogy of being (the necessary and grounding relation of all beings to the One), found less and less space to grow and suffuse society with a more humane approach to societal relations. The true vision that the "Angelic Doctor" had developed of the greatness and inviolability of humanity through his anthropological categories cited above, rather than his isolated and bewildering moralization on sick members and amputations, became stunted, or perhaps, forgotten for the next six and a half centuries.

The rise of Nominalism, with the consequences mentioned above, and the Protestant Reformation, which built on the Nominalist vision, unleashed a veritable bloodbath of capital punishment. Megivern's account of the brutal and ever-intensifying executions decreed by papal mandate from the pontificate of Nicholas V (1447-1455) to Clement VIII (1592-1605) is inclusive and thoroughly researched. Of particular horror were the reigns of Sixtus V (1585-1590) and Clement. Under the latter, Giordano Bruno suffered execution at the stake in Rome's Campo di Fiori, on February 17, 1600, after seven years of incarceration and repeated tortures to make him recant.

Similarly in England, Elizabeth I (1556-1603) had over 124 Catholic priests and Protestant ministers put to death for their faith. The common form of death meted out to these "heretics" was the punishment reserved for traitors: first they would be hanged; then the rope would be cut-off just before death; next the prisoner would be stretched on a block, disemboweled alive, his intestines shown to him, and burned before his eyes; finally, the executioner would pluck the heart out and quarter the body.

This brutality was equaled in some Roman executions, like that of Pomponio de Algerio di Nola, who on August 19, 1556, during the pontificate of Paul IV (1555-1559), was immersed in a cauldron of boiling oil for denying the sacraments and papal authority.

Martin Luther (1483-1546) and Jean Calvin (1509-1564) also validated the death penalty for religious and political opponents. Luther's crusade of 1525 against Thomas Muntzer's Anabaptists resulted in the massacre of over 25,000 peasants. On October 27, 1556, the physician Michel Servet died in Geneva, burned alive at the stake by order of Calvin.

The influence of Nominalist philosophy on Catholic Neo-Scholastic theologians of the post-Reformation and Baroque periods, intensified by apologetic urgency to confront Reformation theology, brought about a prepositional systematization of theology where the dynamics of the biblical and patristic theologies of grace and nature were dismissed in favor of conceptualistic understandings of Jesus, the Church and Christian life.

The theory of "pure nature," a humanity understood as created for a "purely natural finality" to which God added a "grace of elevation" to a supernatural end, replaced the common understanding of the Tradition from Augustine to Thomas Aquinas, whereby the human person has a single finality to God, that grounds and validates the person's dignity and worth in terms of human nature. The concept of "pure nature" gave rise to a separation, in theological texts, between grace and nature, faith and reason, human freedom and divine will. The wonderful dignity of the human person rooted in his/her sealed image of God begins to fade, in favor of a reified notion of humanity.

Within this order of things, God becomes, however subconsciously, more and more remote. A deprecation of the Church's mission is a logical concomitant. Within two and a half-centuries, the rationalism of the modern European Enlightenment, with its mechanistically deist understanding of God as a remote and impersonal clockmaker, and finally the dawn of a philosophically systematic atheism already represented by Denise Diderot, completed the Nominalists' separation of God from the world.

Yet out of all this there would paradoxically emerge strong humanistic and secular arguments against the death penalty that Church law, doctrine and theology had so frighteningly established.

FROM CESARE BECCARIA TO THE CONTEMPORARY SCENE

In 1764, the Italian humanist and social critic Cesare Beccaria (1738-1794) published a work titled *On Crimes and Punishment.* It is difficult to exaggerate the influence of this treatise in later debates on capital punishment. Beccaria has been regarded as the father of the anti-death penalty position, and remains mandatory reading to this day for those involved in the polemical debates on this topic. James Megivern argues that:

> *This ... emphasizes the monumental changes taking place in Christian Europe ... The challenge to its propriety [of the death penalty] would come from ethicists and lawyers, historians and criminologists, Protestant and Catholic, and would come from every country in Europe. Churchmen who simply dug in their heels and held the line against any reassessment actually contributed to the decline of Christianity. The role of custodian of higher values was to be taken up by other forces in support of a more humane ethic.*[5]

The decline of Christianity was indeed, as Megivern argues, part of the great tragedy resulting from the visible, official position of the Christian churches to the abolition of the death penalty, whereas the leaders of the new secular culture – the philosophers and humanists who dismissed or ignored Christian doctrine and principles as disguised superstition, as vestiges of ancient, unsophisticated ages, or worse, as the protectors and guarantors of oppressive governments –

5 Megivern, 214.

became the vanguard of the abolitionist movement. Beccaria's argument pivoted around three points.

1. *The argument regarding usefulness and justice:* The death penalty is neither just nor useful (as deterrent.)
2. *The argument from social theory:* Laws are "the sum of the smallest portion of the private liberty of each individual, and represent the general will, which is the aggregate of each individual. Did anyone ever give to others the right of taking away his life? … If it were so, how shall it be reconciled to the maxim, which tells us that a human has no right to kill oneself? Which one certainly must have, if one could give it away to another."
3. *The argument from human rights:* There exists no right to inflict punishment by death upon anyone. This is a course of "a war of a whole nation against a citizen."

Beccaria's initiative, an opening salvo by modernity against the absurdity of the death penalty, was echoed by contemporary and later thinkers. Voltaire (1694-1778) appealed for mercy in three cases of capital sentencing, and in general deemed the whole history of the West as a succession of gallows where thousands of people were denied mercy.

In general, there were few echoes after Beccaria. Immanuel Kant (1724-1804) would make the death penalty necessary, intimately bound with the logic of his categorical imperatives. The paradigm for future Catholic moralists, St. Alphonsus Liguori integrated the death penalty into his apologetics of the faith, thus perpetuating the medieval support of it.

A few, infrequent voices within the Catholic communion emerged in the period between the French Revolution (1789) and the First Vatican Council. The Belgian Jean-Joseph Thonissen (1816-1891) and the Italian Pietro Ellero (1833-1933) argued against the morality and the practicality of the death penalty. Some Catholic voices began to synthesize in true Catholic fashion both the best theological tradition of the Church and the humanistic voices of the Enlightenment. But, by and large, these Catholic voices did not represent the official teaching of the Church at the time. Rome perceived with suspicion theologians like the Tubinger scholar Johann Adam Moehler (1796-1838). In fact, some of these voices, also raised for Church reform, experienced rejection and repression from Pius IX (1846-1878); among other instances, the Pope condemned the reform-minded congress of Catholic intellectuals in Munich in 1863 through the Bull *Tuas Libenter*, a forerunner of Pius X's *Lamentabili* and *Pascendi* of 1907.

The period from Vatican I to Vatican II (1962-1965) found a few voices emerging, first feebly, then louder. But Catholic Neo-Scholastic philosophers and theologians of the nineteenth century, such as Matteo Liberatore, Joseph Kleutgen (who had been influential in Vatican I), and others had advocated the validity of the death penalty for the same reason that popes during the Enlightenment and the early Romantic period had: the arguments against it came from philosophers and humanitarians marginal to the Church's orthodoxy, and not infrequently hostile to it. The defense of the death penalty continued to be an essential element of the overall apologetics of the Church's teaching.

Contemporary Catholic Rejection of the Death Penalty

Situated amidst the current controversies about the death penalty in the United States, we may begin this last section by recalling the evolution of the debate over the death penalty among Catholics in the U.S. The influence of American anti-death penalty figures like Benjamin Rush, Edward Livingston and Walt Whitman would surely bear upon later Catholic thinkers, and they deserve to be taken into account, but our initial concentration will be on the U.S. Catholic Church.

The emergence of the American church from a church of mission to full self-standing status in 1908 gave American intellectual voices a broader space for discussion. The early edition of *The Catholic Encyclopedia* reflected the standard Catholic teaching on the defensibility of the death penalty. The apologetic mind had not grown of age yet. Anti-Catholicism was still rife in the U.S., and the Catholic faith, according to its apologists, had to be defended *in toto*, without negotiating away any part of it.

Catholic attention was drawn, however, to three cases where judicial procedure, according to historical evidence, may have been infringed, resulting, most probably, in executions of innocents. Sacco and Vanzetti (1927), Bruno Hauptmann (1936), and Julius and Ethel Rosenberg (1953) polarized feelings of xenophobia and juridical expediousness rather than justice.

Yet it was Europe that took the lead in abolishing capital punishment: Denmark, Spain, England, and France all followed the very early example of Portugal, which celebrated its centenary of abolition in 1967. This year also witnessed the national moratorium on executions in the United States, as well as a revised edition of *The Catholic Encyclopedia* with a more nuanced view of the death penalty, stopping just short of deeming it unethical.

The American bishops' "turnaround" began shortly afterwards. In 1972 the Indiana bishops and other state Episcopal conferences began to advocate abolition. The United States Catholic Conference/National Council of Catholic Bishops meeting of 1974, however, did not come to an agreement on the rejection of the death penalty. Again, some, like Cardinal Carberry of St. Louis, raised the apologetics question.

But the movement of reform would not be denied. Following the resumption within the United States of legal executions in 1977, with the willing death by firing squad of Gary Gilmore in Utah, Catholic bishops, theologians and lay leaders pursued a more committed path. In 1979 Florida's Catholic bishops protested the execution of John

Spenkelink, and similar Episcopal interventions occurred in following years. For the period from 1984 to the present, marked by a large number of Episcopal statements, the reader may consult Megivern's massive collection of data.

Finally, recent statements by Pope John Paul II against the death penalty witness to a radical shift in the Catholic attitude toward capital punishment. This shift may also be seen in the changes made in the appropriate texts of the *Catechism of the Catholic Church*, as well as the pope's powerful reflections in his major Encyclical letter *Evangelium Vitae.*

Thus we see the complex history of the shifting development of Catholic social teaching on the death penalty: first, a centuries-old tradition of granting it political and ecclesiastical space for the sake of combating heresy; later, its defense as a mode of guarding the whole of the faith against the perceived dangers of secularism and rationalism; still later cautious utterances against its usefulness; and finally the Catholic tradition arriving late at the crossroads of history but still arriving, nevertheless.

In their current Catholic teaching against the death penalty, the pope and bishops have chosen a truly prophetic stance, drawn from the courage of the prophets of Israel, and from the risky, dangerous memory of Jesus of Nazareth's demands for love and forgiveness.

Concluding Reflection

The persistent defense of the death penalty found for so long in the Christian church's teaching until recent years makes us pause. What sort of moral and theological contamination has the teaching of Jesus of Nazareth, as epitomized in the Sermon on the Mount, suffered through the centuries, as political power, economic wealth, and cultural prestige all beclouded the prophetic vision that the Christian community had been called to since its first gathering around the person of the Messiah? In response to this question, allow me to offer two tentative answers.

First, Christians, including Catholic Christians, called to preach the freedom of the baptized from fear and prejudice (cf. John 14:1, 27; Isaiah 41:8-10; 43: 1-3; 44: 1-3), have indeed succumbed, time and again, to that fear. Fear of humanity's intrinsic worth as the playground of grace, as loved by God, sinful and all, *for its own sake.* Christians fall time and again in the *peccatum originale originans* (originating original sin), as St. Augustine put it – a mistrust of our own humanity, of our own creatureliness. The men and women of the Church feel the urge time and again to be like God. Isn't the original and ultimate temptation of Jesus: "Covert the stones into bread "(Matthew 4:3)? "Come down from the Cross, if indeed you are the Messiah, the Son of God: (Matthew 27: 42-43)? Despair of your humanity, Jesus is told; play to be God. So too Christians are tempted to forget that it is the inviolable, precious, awesome dignity of the human person that has always been, is now, and forever will be the locus of salvation.

Second, I believe that Christians have always been more tempted by religious arrogance, manipulation and selfishness than by "secular" sins. The latter need not mean a fundamental option against the Gospel (although, obviously, sometimes they are); the former almost always reflects a way of life not necessarily perverted in itself, but worse than that, indifferent to the call for holiness. "Go and sell all your possessions, sell them to the poor, and then come and follow me" remains the so-often unmet challenge.

The future of Christianity's life and teaching, including the stance of Catholic Christians against the death penalty, will be contingent on how much we REALLY mean to follow Jesus Christ, poor and despised, displaying through his wounds the glorious dignity of being human and un-killable, or how much we will choose the death wish of wealth, power, and oppression.

We pray to the Heart of Jesus for light, love and forgiveness.

8

THOMAS AQUINAS ON THE DEATH PENALTY

ROBERT VALLE, PH.D.
Assistant Professor of Philosophy
Saint John Vianney College Seminary, Miami, Florida

There is an old story told of a town in southern Germany at the time of the Counter-Reformation. This town had "gone Protestant" during the time of the Reformation and then "repented" of its lapse when it was taken over again by a Catholic prince. Rome sent a papal legate to sort out the situation. After spending a few weeks there, the legate wrote back to Rome for directions. He was very frustrated. He claimed that it seemed that almost everyone had apostatized during the period of Protestant rule, but it was not a very sincere brand of apostasy. They had done so only to save their skins. And now everyone was Catholic again. But, again, it seemed not too sincere. They only wished to be on the side of the secular power. The cardinal in Rome reportedly, and one can only hope apocryphally, wrote back to the legate: "Kill them all and God will know his own."

Whether it has any historical foundation or not, this story takes us to the roots of the Catholic struggle with the death penalty. As many Catholics know, great thinkers in the Catholic tradition have allowed use of the death penalty. However, the flippant disregard for human life, implicit in the cardinal's reply, is surely not part of the Christian tradition. First, the death penalty is not considered by either Augustine or Aquinas in the cool and dispassionate air of calm reflection – Aquinas' cool and dispassionate prose notwithstanding. In both instances – the 5th and 13th centuries – the church is racked by the problem of heresy. Second, the death penalty is not considered, as it would be today, as the exclusive prerogative of the secular government. Indeed, it was part of an innately theological discussion as to how to deal with heretics. Third, as is obvious in both Augustine and Aquinas, each great thinker struggled with the tensions involved, neither was blithely or entirely at ease with this final solution for heresy.

Saint Thomas Aquinas, and to a lesser degree Saint Augustine,[1] approve of the use of the death penalty under certain conditions and for certain reasons. However, to simply say that they were "for" the death penalty with no further qualifications or limitations is, while technically accurate, a highly distorted view of their positions.

This chapter seeks to investigate the specifically Thomistic view of the death penalty. It will focus on the treatment of the death penalty

---

1 James Megivern, *The Death Penalty, An Historical and Theological Survey* (New York: Paulist Press 1997), 35-44; *n.b.,* Megivern points out the ambivalent nature of Augustine's position on the death penalty. The early Augustine is firmly against it. It is only after witnessing the good that Roman arms do in fighting heresy that Augustine reluctantly allows the death penalty. However, Augustine never loses his fierce pastoral focus, which is to say, while he admits that the state has the theoretical right to take a life, he is loath to ever see that right exercised in practice. *Cf.* Garry Wills, *Saint Augustine* (New York: A Viking Book, 1999), 109-112; Wills shows that even the latter Augustine is not at all comfortable with capital punishment: "When the murderers of his priest confessed, Augustine showed what he meant by discipline as a teaching instrument. He begged Marcellinus not to execute, maim, or flog the men (customary Roman penalties)"[109-110]. Marcellinus replied that he could not give such assurances. Whereupon Augustine replied, "As for us, if no lighter sentence were available, we should prefer to see them released rather than avenge our brother's murder by further bloodshed" [110]. Augustine even goes so far as to inform Marcellinus that he was instigating a plea for clemency directly to the emperor.

in the *Summa Contra Gentiles* and the *Summa Theologiae.* It will pass over in silence the treatment to be found in the *Commentary on the Sentences of Peter Lombard* because this text does not contain the mature thought of Thomas on the matter and contains almost nothing original. In general, the chapter will agree with the work of Brian Calvert (1992), which holds that "there is a more than even chance that if Aquinas were alive today he might well turn out to be an abolitionist."[2]

This chapter will investigate the texts of St. Thomas on the death penalty and then explore the context of Thomistic thought in general. The argument that Thomas today might well be an abolitionist in terms of the death penalty can rest on the texts or the context. The textual argument would search for weaknesses in the texts themselves, being especially cognizant of moments when the Thomistic texts seem to be somewhat at odds with Thomistic thought in general. The contextual argument would claim that Thomas could indeed have been for the death penalty in the thirteenth century and yet, by his own logic, against the death penalty in the twenty-first century due to the fact that the historical context has dramatically changed.

The *Summa Contra Gentiles* does not take up the question of the death penalty until Book III, chapter 144. Then, it is within the context of asking whether mortal sin deprives a man of his ultimate end: *Quid per peccatum mortale ultimo fine aliquis in aeternum priviatur?*.[3] Article nine of chapter 144 is of crucial importance for understanding the Thomistic position. Thomas anticipates his medicinal argument, "the

---

2 Brian Calvert, "Aquinas and the Death Penalty," *The American Journal of Jurisprudence* (Washington), 37 (November, 1992): 259-281.

3 Thomas Aquinas, *Summa Contra Gentiles,* translated by Vernon Bourke (Notre Dame: University of Notre Dame Press, 1997), c. 144, henceforth SCG.

punishments under human law are applied for the remedy of vices, and so they are like medicines."[4]

Hence, punishments have no intrinsic value. It is immoral to punish for punishment's sake, as in cases of revenge or spite. To punish for punishment's sake is, moreover, impossible for the Divine being, for such vindictive punishment would be incommensurate with divine goodness. Instead: "Punishments must be inflicted for the sake of something else."[5] This passage provides the key to what Aquinas has to say about punishment, and conditions all of his subsequent reflections on the matter.

The purpose of punishment always resides in some proximate goal. Punishment restores a lost order, actually a three-fold order: the order of the individual human being, the social order and the divine order. For this reason, the first response is to attempt to correct the sinner (heretic) so that all three orders may be restored. However, failure on the level of the individual sinner does not mean that punishment is no longer appropriate or justifiable. Should the conversion succeed, Aquinas would seem to hold that no further punishment would be necessary, being that all three levels could then be restored.[6]

It is still possible that, "the wicked man being scourged, the fool shall be wiser."[7] Hence, the social order may be redeemable even if the personal order is not. This position will be re-stated and somewhat clarified in the *Summa Theologiae*, I-II, Q. 87, art. 1.

Thomas goes further. Where divine punishment is at stake, the order restored is the order of divine justice: "Now we have to concede that

---

4 SCG, c. 144, art. 9, cf. "*enim humanis legibus inferuntur ad emendationen vitiorum: unde sicut medicinae quaedum sunt.*"

5 SCG, c. 144, art 9; cf. "*Oportet igitur poenas propter aliud inferri.*"

6 The personal order is made right. The fool sees that the reform has done well and so he learns. The divine order of justice, upon which the good of the universe depends, is demarcated and affirmed as the true and proper order.

7 SCG, c.144, art. 11; cf., "*Pestilente flaggellato, stultus sapientior erit.*"

punishments are not inflicted by God for their own sake, as if God delighted in them, but are there for something else; namely, for the imposing of order on creatures, in which the good of the universe consists."[8] Hence, punishment is possible even when no personal or social advantage accrues from it. The order of the divine justice, upon which the good of the universe depends, is thus maintained and strengthened.

Hence, Thomas concludes that punishments are not merely meted out so as to correct behavior: "Nothing prevents some people, according to divine judgment, from having to be separated perpetually from the society of good men and to be punished eternally."[9]

This conclusion is somewhat uncharacteristic of Thomas. It shows little of his typical nuance and balance. It is rare that anywhere in Thomas one finds a position so seemingly single-minded. This is hard to explain from the sources available to us. In fact, many Thomistic commentators have struggled mightily with attempting to explain this rather facile logic.[10]

In chapter 146, art. 4 of the *Summa Contra Gentiles*, Thomas reiterates, "certain men must be removed by death from the society of men."[11] Then, Thomas offers the famous analogy of the diseased organ: "Now the physician quite properly and beneficially cuts off a diseased organ if the corruption of the body is threatened because of it.

---

8 SCG, c. 144, art. 10; cf., "*Est autem concedendum quod poenae inferuntur a Deo non propter se, quasi Deus in ipsis delectetur, sed propter aliud: scilicet propter ordinem imponedum creaturis, in quo bonum universi consistit.*"

9 SCG, c. 144, art. 11; cf., "*Nihil igitur prohibet...quin, secundum divinum iudicium, aliqui debeant a societate bonorum perpetuo separari et in aeternum puniri.*"

10 The Blackfriars English/Latin edition of the text of the *Summa Theologica* is quick to qualify the article on heresy [ST, 2a2ae II, 3] by claiming: "This article can only be appreciated when its historical period is kept in mind" [p. 89].

11 SCG, 146, art. 4; cf., "*igitur sunt huismodi homines per mortem ab hominum societate.*"

Therefore, the ruler of a state executes pestiferous men justly and sinlessly in order that the peace of the state may not be disrupted."[12]

It is difficult to understand how Thomas, the great wielder of distinctions, could have failed to make a distinction between the manner in which a gangrenous arm is related to the body and how the sinner is related to the social order. Surely, such a distinction is necessary. Even given the fact that medieval theologians made liberal use of this analogy of Church as body and sinner as gangrenous limb, it is clear that the sinner is not related to the Church, as the limb is to the body in a literal or even univocal sense.

In articles 6, 7 and 8 of this chapter, Thomas rehearses the traditional pastoral argument against capital punishment, an argument made by Augustine and St. John Chrysostom. The argument interprets the parable of the tares and the wheat (Matthew 13) to mean that the Church should tolerate heretics. In an unprecedented and shocking move, Thomas does not answer the objections but concludes at the start of article 9, "these arguments are frivolous."[13] Thomas, of course, does not always agree with Augustine but he always takes him seriously. To dismiss his saintly predecessor as "frivolous" is a striking singularity in the thought of Aquinas: "One gets the impression that something has spoiled the conversation here. Aquinas does not look any further than the latest source of these arguments, the condemned heretics of the previous generation [the Waldensians], taking little note of the otherwise significant fact that highly respected Christian forebears found these arguments entirely persuasive rather than 'frivolous.'"[14]

Article 10 reveals a still more incongruent element. Thomas concludes: "And if they are so stubborn that even at the point of death

---

12 SCG, c. 146, art. 4; cf., "*Medicus autem abscindit membrum putridum bene et utiliter, si per ipsum immmineat corruptio corporis. Iuste igitur et absque peccato rector civitatis homines pestiferos occidit, ne pax civitatis turbetur.*"

13 SCG, c. 146; art. 9; cf., "*Haec autem frivola sunt.*"

14 Megivern, *The Death Penalty*, 116.

their heart does not draw back from evil, it is possible to make a highly probable judgment that they would never come away from evil to the right use of their powers."[15] This passage is completely amazing and unique for Thomas. The great Doctor of grace has suddenly concluded that it "is highly probable" that some heretics are in such a state of perversion that they are virtually immune to grace. It is difficult to see how one could reconcile this conclusion to Thomas' thought in general.

One might conclude that in the turbulent and pre-Inquisitional atmosphere of the thirteenth century, the matter was deeply obscured by polemics, even for one so brilliant as Thomas. The traditional commentators on St. Thomas have tended to gloss over the weaknesses in the text. For example, Gilson summarizes: "And just as a surgeon has to cut off a gangrenous member in order to save a man's life, it can be necessary to cut off a member of society if its corruption is a menace to the social body."[16] No mention is made here, or anywhere else in Gilson's magisterial work, of the theological context of the discussion, the blithe dismissal of Augustine, or the possibility that separation from the society of men might not require death. If some lesser means is possible, given the seriousness involved with the shedding of human blood, would it not be worth investigating? It is almost as if even Thomas' friends are a bit embarrassed.

The *Summa Theologiae* gives an expanded treatment of the issue, though the fundamental position is essentially unchanged. PT II-II, q. 11, art 3, shows that Thomas is much more explicit as to the necessarily theological grounds of capital punishment. Heretics, after proving repeatedly unrepentant, "deserve not only to be separated from the Church by excommunication but also to be severed from the world by death. For it is a much graver matter to corrupt the faith which quickens the soul, than to forge money, which supports

---

15 SCG, c. 146, art. 10; cf., "*Quod si adeo sunt obstinati quod etiam in mortis articulo cor eorum a malitia non recedit, satis probabiliter aestimari potest quod nunquam a malitia.*"

16 Etienne Gilson, *The Christian Philosophy of St. Thomas Aquinas*, translated by L.K. Shook (New York: Random House, 1956), 313.

temporal life."[17] Heresy is viewed as the sin that most properly merits the ultimate penalty.

Moreover, Thomas is clear that while the heretic is executed in the name of the Church, it should never be the cleric who executes. The Church disciplines, and only when correction fails, and fails repeatedly, is the miscreant excommunicated and delivered "to the secular tribunal to be exterminated thereby from the world by death."[18] In short, the Church's first and best goal is not death but the conversion of the heretic whereby all three orders – the personal, the social and the divine – are restored.

Also relevant here is the reference to the fact that the "secular authority" performs the actual killing. Any cleric who performed such killing would be canonically liable to be deposed and even the layperson would incur an irregularity resulting from any taking of life whatsoever. Even the judge who imposes a lawful sentence or a soldier in battle at the time of Aquinas would be tainted with this irregularity. Moreover, the canonical code claimed that this impediment is a perpetual one and thereby is an irregularity.[19]

The most significant changes in canonical thought on this issue since the time of Thomas are that the prohibition is somewhat muted in terms of its applicability and expanded in terms of its scope. Which is to say, first, that the current Code allows for the exception of legitimate homicide: "Death resulting from an accident or legitimate

---

17 Thomas Aquinas, *Summa Theologica*, translated by the Fathers of the English Dominican Province (New York: Benziger, 1947) Vol. 2, 1226, henceforth, ST; *cf.* "*non solum ab Ecclesia per exommunicationem separari, sed etiam per mortem a mundo excludi. Multo enim gravius est corrumpere fidem, per quam est animæ vita, quam falsare pecuniam, per quam temporalia vitæ subvenitur.*"

18 ST, II-II, Q. 11, art. 3; cf., "*et ulterius relinquit eum judicio sæculari a mundo exterminandum per mortem.*"

19 This term "irregularity" does not mean that the impediment cannot be dispensed with but only that it is never removed and must indeed be dispensed.

self defense is not a cause of irregularity."[20] Second, as canon 1397 of the current Code states, "One who commits homicide.... is to be punished with the deprivation and prohibitions mentioned in canon 1336."[21] As is evident, the distinction between the cleric, who must keep his hands free of blood, and the layperson, who may and must sully them, has been greatly blurred, perhaps erased. Notice the canon covers cleric and laity: "The revised law ... neither differentiates between clergy and laity nor refers to a civil law condemnation."[22]

Thomas allows the death penalty for the explicit purpose of dealing with heresy, and then the ecclesiastical authority would act through the instrumental causation of the secular authority. The situation today is drastically changed. The civil authority does not act in accord with the ecclesiastical authority. Hence, the secular power has no pastoral solicitude for the sinner, nor any desire or mandate to convert the sinner. It is highly doubtful that Thomas would have seen the death penalty as justifiable in such a bifurcated context. Furthermore, it is not merely a matter of giving the sinner a few chances before killing him or her. It is a matter of seriously desiring and striving to restore the order of goodness at the personal level. The modern state is neither equipped for, nor desirous of, serving such a role.

Aquinas is most keenly aware of this difficulty, and, taken together, the canonical irregularity and the change of thought in the 1917 and 1983 Code serve to weaken somewhat Thomas' logic. The *Summa Theologiae* states that it is unlawful for a cleric to kill, "first they are chosen for service of the altar...the other reason is because clerics are entrusted with the ministry of the New Law, wherein no punishment of death or of bodily maiming is appointed: wherefore they [clerics] should abstain from such things in order that they may be fitting

---

20 *The Code of Canon Law, a Text and Commentary* (New York: Paulist Press, 1985), 730, henceforth, Code of Canon Law.

21 *Code of Canon Law*, 930.

22 Ibid.

ministers of the New Testament."[23] As is clearly and forcefully stated in Vatican II's Dogmatic Constitution on the Church, *Lumen Gentium*, priesthood essentially belongs to the whole people of God by virtue of baptism. Hence, as ministers of the New Law which allows no punishment of death or bodily maiming, we should all abstain from such actions.

As has been shown above, the texts of Thomas are complex and problematic on many levels. Hence, it would not seem possible to affirm in any simplistic sense that Thomas was for the death penalty. Moreover, again as seen above, it may be that Thomas' position on this matter is not entirely consistent with the style or content of Thomistic thought in general. Nevertheless, even if one were to contest these theses, it is still possible and necessary to consider that if Thomas were alive today, he would be an abolitionist in terms of the death penalty.

Punishment, for Thomas, has no intrinsic value. The death penalty, if it is justifiable, is only justifiable because it accrues to some proximate end, actually to three specific proximate ends: the individual order of goodness, the social order of goodness, and the divine order of justice upon which the good of the universe depends [ST, Pars I-II, Q. 87, art. 1]. Given the very serious matter involved with the taking of life [ST, Q. 64, Pars II-II, arts. 1-8], it is necessary that punishment meets these proximate goals, so as to justify killing. So, even if Thomas were for capital punishment in the thirteenth century, would he be for it in the twenty-first? The answer to that question depends on whether capital punishment meets these proximate goals. Does it preserve the order of the good in the individual? Does it preserve the order of the good in society? Does it preserve the order of divine justice upon which the good of the universe depends?

---

23 ST, II-II, Q. 64, art 4; cf., "Primo quidem quia sunt electi ad altaris ministerium...Secundum judicem populi, sic et ministri ejus. Alia ratio est, quia clericis committitur ministerium novæ legis, in qua non-determinatur pœna occisionis vel mutilationis corporalis. Et ideo ut sint idonei ministri novi Testmenti, debent a talibus abstinere."

Obviously, capital punishment does not restore the order of the good in the individual. In fact, infliction of the death penalty implies that we have despaired that the person ever reforms. Aquinas was cognizant of this fact, as is evident in his reasoning that the soul separated from its body could never achieve its final end, insofar as the soul requires the body to attain its proper perfection.

However, the "Angelic Doctor" held that the social order was restored since the fool, seeing the wicked scourged, would grow wiser. The question here is not a logical one but a practical one: is society better because of the use of capital punishment? When the fool sees the wicked punished, is the fear of God put into him, does he grow wiser? The answer today would seem to be, "no." In the first place,

> *the vast preponderance of the evidence shows that the death penalty is no more effective than imprisonment in deterring murder and that it may even be an incitement to criminal violence. Death-penalty states as a group do not have lower rates of criminal homicide than non-death-penalty states. During the early 1970s, death-penalty states averaged an annual rate of 7.9 criminal homicides per 100,000 population; abolitionist states averaged a rate of 5.1.*[24]

Some have actually argued that the use of the death penalty in a given state may actually increase the subsequent rate of criminal homicide. In Oklahoma, for example, reintroduction of executions in 1990 may have produced "an abrupt and lasting increase in the level of stranger homicides" in the form of "one additional stranger-homicide incident per month." Why? Perhaps because "a return to the exercise of the death penalty weakens socially based inhibitions against the use of lethal force to settle disputes."[25]

In adjacent states – one with the death penalty and the other without it – the state that practices the death penalty does not show a consis-

---

24 See *Uniform Crime Reports*, 1993, and note 2 et seq.

25 Cochran, Chamlin and Seth. "Deterrence or Brutalization?" In *Criminology* (1994).

tently lower rate of criminal homicide. For example, between 1990 and 1994, the homicide rates in Wisconsin and Iowa (non-death penalty states) were half the rates of their neighbor, Illinois – which restored the death penalty in 1973, and by 1994, had sentenced 223 persons to death and carried out two executions.[26]

Hence, the social order, far from being restored, may be actually positively harmed by capital punishment. States that practice the death penalty appear to be more violent than others that do not. Hence, the first two proximate goals of capital punishment seem not to be attained; that is, the human order is demolished, with no hope of redemption, and the social order is positively harmed.

The third level, the order of divine justice, upon which the good of the universe depends, is not even at stake in the modern discussion. The modern state does not presume to speak in the name of divine justice. If the modern state is going to make an argument for its rightful use of capital punishment, it is going to have to do so within the immanent realm of rights, duties and obligations and not by some appeal to transcendent or theological justifications.

Thomas' view of the death penalty, and his view of punishment in general, is thoroughly consequentialist in nature. He explicitly holds that punishment for the sake of revenge, spite, or even pure retribution is morally wrong and inadmissible. Hence, modern theories, which justify the death penalty as some form of retribution, are very far from the mind of Thomas.

In the final analysis, Thomas would ask if, given the seriousness involved with the taking of a life, would there not be some other way in which these proximate goals could be met, especially if they are not even being presently met by capital punishment. The fact that Thomas Aquinas, one of the greatest questioners in the history of the West, did not even consider this possibility points not to the fact

---

26 U.S. Bureau of Justice Statistics, *Death Row Statistics. 1996* (Washington D.C.), 7-8.

that Thomas was in any way a dullard or a coward. Thomas, who looked at every question from seemingly every side, does not consider the most obvious possible alternatives. This is due, I think, to the raging polemical fires of his day and the pervasive, creeping tide of the Inquisition, which would drown all Europe in its bitter wake. As Megivern holds, "Capital punishment was by this time so firmly entrenched, especially for dealing with obstinate heretics, that it was shielded from serious criticism, even from one so astute as Aquinas."[27]

There is no significant reason to presume that Thomas Aquinas in the twenty-first century would be any more for the death penalty than he would for his Aristotelian biology (e.g., that a girl is conceived if a wind is blowing from the south and a boy if the wind is blowing from the north during conception, or that a woman is an imperfect man). In short, the Thomistic doctrine of the death penalty was a result of his time, as was his faulty biology. His own texts, read interpretively and consistently, point toward abolition of the death penalty and not its perpetuation.

27 Megivern, *The Death Penalty*, 118.

9

CATHOLIC TEACHING AGAINST THE DEATH PENALTY

CLIVE DILLON-MALONE, S.J., PH.D.
Chairperson, Department of Philosophy & Applied Ethics
University of Zambia, Lusaka, Zambia

The following paper was first given at the Catholic Commission for Justice and Peace Conference on the Death Penalty held at Mulungushi International Conference Centre on September 2, 2000 and was later reproduced in two issues of THE CHALLENGE, a Catholic magazine published in Zambia.

The teaching of the Catholic Church today is moving closer and closer toward a total rejection of capital punishment for even the most vile of criminals.[1] This was not always the case, for there has been a significant development in the Church's social teaching in fairly recent times. In the past, the death penalty for murderers in particular was justified by the Church in certain circumstances, and it must be acknowledged that there is a strand of the Church's teaching that has supported capital punishment. However, the Church is now moving away from that position.

1 Although the death penalty may be inflicted for crimes other than murder, such as treason, rape, torture, kidnapping, etc., for purposes of convenience, I will be referring primarily to murder in this paper with reference to capital punishment.

Before commenting on the modern position of the Catholic Church on capital punishment, it will help to outline briefly some of the theories that have been put forward on criminal punishment.

Theories of Criminal Punishment

There are many theories about punishment in the case of criminal behaviour, and these theories look at capital punishment from different points of view. The most important of these theories are retributive theory and utilitarian theory. Other theories that contain variations on these are natural-law theory,[2] natural-rights theory[3] and contractarian theory.[4] It will help to look briefly at key aspects of retributive theory and utilitarian theory in particular.

The Retributive Theory of Punishment

Although there are different versions of this theory, it basically states that wrongdoing deserves punishment in proportion to the wrong done. Punishment is justified because the offender has voluntarily committed a wrong act. This theory focuses its attention on the past

---

2 In natural-law theory, justice is the habit of rendering each person his or her due. Reward is due to those who act rightly in society and punishment is due to those who act wrongly.

3 Natural-rights theory states that the aim of punishment is to protect people's rights. Punishment is therefore justified because the criminal has interfered with the rights of others. In such cases, criminals are believed to forfeit some of their natural rights. The problem with this theory is that it is not always clear in many cases whether the rights of the victim or of the offender should prevail and which rights the offender should forfeit.

4 Contractarian theory supports an impartial system of legal justice with a strong emphasis on protecting the liberty of the innocent. Proportionate punishment for the wrong done must be combined with an assessment of the culpability of the wrongdoer and suffering should be as minimal as possible to ensure the effectiveness of deterrence. Punishment is permissible, though not necessary; and it should be proportional to the wrong done, though not necessarily equal.

wrong actions of the criminal. People are morally responsible for their actions and guilt deserves punishment. The suffering which the criminal undergoes is not bad in itself in this case and it is justly inflicted whether or not it results in any good consequences. This is referred to as "*lex talionis*," the law of retaliation, "an eye for an eye and a tooth for a tooth." In some way or another, the moral balance has been upset and proportionate punishment is necessary to restore this balance. Private vengeance is avoided by having the state judge the crime and administer the punishment. The retributivist theory rests on a theory of justice in which punishment is understood as the just desert for a crime.

The Utilitarian Theory of Punishment

Although there are different versions of this theory also, it basically states that punishment is justified solely in terms of its good consequences. This theory focuses on the future. Punishment is, therefore, considered bad in itself and to be justified only if it prevents ever-greater suffering or if it brings about greater good. The innocence or guilt of the concerned party is not the prime concern of the utilitarian as the chief aim of punishment is to reduce crime.

Punishment is intended by the utilitarian to bring about one or all of the following results:

- to act as a deterrent to prevent the criminal from committing future crimes;
- to act as a deterrent on others who might be contemplating a similar crime;
- to protect others in society from the threat of the criminal;
- to help to reform the criminal.

The problem with the utilitarian theory is that the deterrent effect of capital punishment has been severely questioned.[5] In recent times,

---

5 The Royal Commission on Capital Punishment (1949-53), having weighed the

therefore, greater emphasis has been placed on the importance of rehabilitating the criminal so that both the criminal and society at large will benefit. It should be noted, however, that reform of the criminal is not an assured result from punishment. In fact, the opposite may be the case. However, reformative measures can accompany punishment in such a way that they can provide the conditions for reform of the criminal. For instance, the loss of freedom may provide the opportunity for reflection and moral change.

Religious Approaches

Different Religious Traditions

Religious traditions ground their beliefs on their sacred books. Muslims turn to their interpretation of the Koran. Jews turn to the books of the Law and the Prophets in what Christians refer to as the Old Testament. Christians turn to both the Old and the New Testaments with the primary focus on the teaching of Christ in the New Testament.

Christians, however, are not unanimous in their interpretation of their sacred books, and the Catholic Church differs in many respects from other Christian traditions. In particular, the Catholic Church rejects a fundamentalist and literalist interpretation of its sacred books. What this means is that the Catholic Church recognizes advances made by scripture scholars in various fields of linguistic and socio-cultural analysis and acknowledges the complex nature of revelation in interpreting God's word as filtered through the medium of a specific human language and culture. Consequently, it interprets the Word of God within the context of the whole life and teaching of Christ and not in terms of the literal interpretation of individual texts or passages of scripture alone. It also recognizes the inseparable link

---

statistical evidence, concluded that it was important "'not to base a penal policy in relation to murder on exaggerated estimates of the uniquely deterrent force of the death penalty'." Cmd. 8932, § 790 (3).

between Scripture and Tradition because the understanding of the life and teaching of Christ by his followers was only committed to writing in the New Testament by the early Christian communities from about thirty years after the death of Christ.

Non-Catholic Interpretations of Scripture

In Genesis 9:6, we read: "He who sheds man's blood shall have his blood shed by man,[6] for in the image of God man was made." And in Exodus 21:12, we read: "Anyone who strikes a man and so causes his death, must die." Here we find clear statements of the Old Testament moral code of *lex talionis*, "life for life, eye for eye, tooth for tooth, hand for hand, foot for foot" (Deuteronomy 19:21). It is a moral code which stipulated that restitution must be paid for a crime of similar proportion to the seriousness of the crime committed. Certain crimes, particularly murder, were seen as so heinous and reprehensible that in justice they demanded a commensurate penalty. The only punishment considered adequate was the death penalty. If a human life is taken, then the life of the killer must be given in return. Only then will justice be fulfilled. This is the Old Testament scriptural basis on which some Christian traditions ground their defense of capital punishment.

This mode of interpretation is further reinforced by the New Testament text found in Romans 13:4 which is taken to refer to the authority believed to be given by God to the state to impose the death penalty: "The state is there to serve God for your benefit. If you break the law, however, you may well have fear: the bearing of the sword has its significance. The authorities are there to serve God: they carry out God's revenge by punishing wrongdoers." The reference to a "sword," in this interpretation, is understood to mean an

---

6 The lack of gender sensitivity in the official English translations of biblical texts is noted. "Man" should be taken to read "human beings." All translations are taken from *The Jerusalem Bible*.

instrument of death, which, in turn, is taken to refer to the death penalty.

Catholic Interpretation of Scripture

The Catholic Church acknowledges that, throughout the history of the chosen people in the Old Testament, there had been a slow process of growth in moral consciousness. God's word was understood and interpreted within the context of social moral standards of the time. Modes of conduct, which today we would consider to be cruel and barbaric, were perpetrated in the name of God. In Numbers 31:7, for instance, we read: "They waged the campaign against Midian, as God ordered Moses, and they put every male to death."[7]

The Catholic Church, however, understands the teaching of Jesus to have superseded biblical texts such as that of Genesis 9:6 when he said: "Do not imagine that I have come to abolish the Law and the Prophets. I have come not to abolish but to complete them." (Matthew 5:17). It understands "the bearing of the sword" by the state in Romans 13:4 to refer not to the necessary infliction of the death penalty, but to the authority of a legitimately appointed state to impose punishment on criminal offenders. For instance, Jesus himself was clearly not referring to killing when he made reference to the sword in Matthew 10:34 with these words: "Do not suppose that I have come to bring peace to the earth: it is not peace I have come to bring but a sword." Again in Ephesians 6:17, we read that you must "receive the word of God from the Spirit to use as a sword."

Political and legal institutions are human-made social structures which differ in different cultures. They are not instituted by God. The laws which they devise are also human-made laws which can and should be developed and changed when necessary. A particular state

---

7 See also Lv. 20:16; 24:21; Nb. 25:5; 35:31; Dt. 13:9; 1 Sam 15:3; and Ezk. 23:47 for similar texts.

may decide to impose the death penalty on murderers, but such a decision is a human-made one and not one mandated by God.

Among the commandments given to Moses was, "You shall not kill" (Exodus 20:13; Deuteronomy 5:17), a command fully endorsed by Jesus himself (Mark 10:19; Mark 19:18). The Church believes that Jesus came to purify and elevate the inhuman moral standards which had been tolerated in Old Testament times. Jesus challenged Old Testament morality whenever he used the words, "You have learnt how it was said ... but I say this to you" (cf. Matthew 5:17-48 *passim*). A particular case in point is Jesus' rejection of the practice of putting people to death. A clear example is found in the case of the woman taken in adultery, for which stoning to death was the socially accepted punishment at the time. Yet Jesus rejected this extreme form of punishment (John 8:3-11).

In Catholic teaching today, there is no scriptural basis in the teaching of Christ for capital punishment. Rather, the life and teaching of Christ focus more explicitly on God's forgiveness and on the call for repentance and conversion on the part of wrongdoers. On the other hand, Christ does not excuse the wrongdoing involved.

THE CATHOLIC CHURCH'S SOCIAL TEACHING

The General Approach

The Catholic Church approaches the issue of the death penalty on its understanding of Scripture and the ongoing tradition of its social moral teaching. While its teaching does not rest on any one particular theory of punishment, it does take cognizance of aspects of different theories.

The Church's social teaching is not static and neither does it develop in a vacuum. As part of a living tradition, it is sensitive to the voice of the Holy Spirit of the Risen Lord as expressed through people of goodwill. This principle was clearly recognized in a document entitled "The Church in the Modern World" in the Catholic Church's most significant event in centuries, *The Second Vatican Council*, which took place from 1963-1965.

The teaching of the Church on capital punishment is, in fact, moving in the same direction as that of the United Nations *Second Optional Protocol to the International Covenant on Civil and Political Rights of 1990,* where it is stated in the prelude that the "abolition of the death penalty contributes to enhancement of human dignity and progressive development of human rights" and that "all measures of abolition of the death penalty should be considered as progress in the enjoyment of the right to life."

Capital punishment cannot be considered on the same level as other forms of punishment on account of its finality. Death is a unique occurrence, which cannot be compared with other events. There is no second chance for the executed. The retributivist theory will say that murderers deserve to die because they have themselves taken a human life. Utilitarians will say that the execution of criminals will act as a deterrent to others. Rights theorists will say that murderers forfeit their right to life. All of these, however, are questionable.

There is no doubt about the fact that murderers deserve to be severely punished. On the other hand, it is not immediately evident that taking their lives restores any moral balance. Neither is there any conclusive evidence that capital punishment acts as a significant deterrent in reducing the incidence of murder in society. It is not clear either that even a murderer can forfeit the right to life if an innocent life is not being directly threatened.

The Catholic Church teaches that every human being has an inalienable right to life. This right to life, however, is not an absolute right in the sense that there can be no circumstances in which this right cannot be overruled. Since every human being has this right to life, an individual who intends to take the life of another human being can forfeit that right. In other words, self-defense is justified in the teaching of the Catholic Church.

Catholic teaching in the past has also allowed the taking of human life in a just war and in capital punishment, although its teaching on these issues are also undergoing change and development in view of the sanctity of every human life, the destructive nature of modern warfare, and developments in criminal justice. What Catholic teaching in recent years has come to call a consistent ethic of life highlights the church's profound concern for human life in the face of abortion, war, euthanasia, and capital punishment.

The Question of Capital Punishment

What, then, is the attitude of the Catholic Church today to the question of capital punishment? In order to approach this question, we need to look at three statements from recent documents of the Catholic Church.

The first is a statement from *The Catechism of the Catholic Church* (1992) of the late Pope John Paul II, which reads as follows:

> *... the traditional teaching of the Church has acknowledged as well-founded the right and duty of legitimate public authority to punish malefactors by means of penalties commensurate with the gravity of the crime, not excluding, in cases of extreme gravity, the death penalty... If bloodless means are sufficient to defend human lives against an aggressor and to protect public order and the safety of persons, public authority should limit itself to such means because they better correspond to the concrete conditions of the common good and are more in conformity to the dignity of the human person.*[8]

The second is the 1995 encyclical of the late Pope John Paul II entitled *The Gospel of Life,* in which the teaching of the church is moved forward quite significantly. The pope sees as one of the encouraging signs of the times in our present society a more widespread reaction against capital punishment:

---

8 §2266, 2267.

> *... there is evidence of a growing public opposition to the death penalty even when such a penalty is seen as a kind of "legitimate defense" on the part of society. Modern society in fact has the means of effectively suppressing crime by rendering criminals harmless without definitively denying them the chance to reform.*[9]

And further on, we read:

> *... on this matter [of the death penalty], there is a growing tendency, both in the Church and in civil society, to demand that it be applied in a very limited way or even that it be abolished completely.... It is clear that for these purposes to be achieved, the nature and extent of the punishment must be carefully evaluated and decided upon, and ought not to go to the extreme of executing the offender except in cases of absolute necessity: in other words, when it would not be possible otherwise to defend society. Today, however, as a result of steady improvements in the organization of the penal system, such cases are very rare, if not practically non-existent.*[10]

---

9 §27.

10 The fuller context of this excerpt is as follows:

> ... on this matter [of the death penalty], there is a growing tendency, both in the Church and in civil society, to demand that it be applied in a very limited way or even that it be abolished completely. The problem must be viewed in the context of a system of penal justice ever more in line with human dignity and thus, in the end, with Gods plan for man [human beings] and society. The primary purpose of the punishment which society inflicts is to redress the disorder caused by the offence. Public authority must redress the violation of personal and social rights by imposing on the offender an adequate punishment for the crime as a condition for the offender to regain the exercise of his or her freedom. In this way, authority also fulfils the purpose of defending public order and ensuring people's safety, while at the same time offering the offender an incentive and help to change his or her behavior and be rehabilitated.
>
> It is clear that for these purposes to be achieved, *the nature and extent of the punishment* must be carefully evaluated and decided upon, and ought not to go to the extreme of executing the offender except in cases of absolute necessity: in other words, when it would not be possible otherwise to defend society. To-

The third is an official amendment, which was made to the *Catechism of the Catholic Church* text in 1997 resulting from the 1995 teaching as mentioned in no. 2 above:

> ... *The traditional teaching of the Church has not excluded recourse to the death penalty ... when this method is the only practicable way to provide an effective defense of human lives against an unjust aggressor. On the other hand, if bloodless means are sufficient to defend human lives against an aggressor and to protect public order and the safety of persons, authority should limit itself to such means, because they better correspond to the concrete conditions of the common good and are more in conformity to the dignity of the human person. Today, in practice... although the possibility is not definitively foreclosed, the cases of absolute necessity for the death of the guilty party are now very rare, if not in practice non-existent.*[11]

The following points should be particularly noted with regard to the texts referred to above:

---

day, however, as a result of steady improvements in the organization of the penal system, such cases are very rare, if not practically non-existent. (§56)

11 The fuller context of this excerpt is as follows:

... the traditional teaching of the Church has acknowledged as well-founded the right and duty of legitimate public authority to punish malefactors by means of penalties commensurate with the gravity of the crime... The traditional teaching of the Church has not excluded recourse to the death penalty on the condition that the identity and responsibility of the guilty party has been clearly demonstrated and when this method is the only practicable way to provide an effective defense of human lives against an unjust aggressor. On the other hand, if bloodless means are sufficient to defend human lives against an aggressor and to protect public order and the safety of persons, authority should limit itself to such means, because they better correspond to the concrete conditions of the common good and are more in conformity to the dignity of the human person. Today, in practice, because of the possibilities open to the state in punishing crimes effectively and rendering harmless those who commit them, although the possibility is not definitively foreclosed, the cases of absolute necessity for the death of the guilty party are now very rare, if not in practice non-existent. (§2266, 2267)

- The death penalty should only be imposed if there is no other "practical way" of defending citizens from unjust aggressors. These practical alternatives are judged to be available in most cases today. "Modern society in fact has the means of effectively suppressing crime by rendering criminals harmless without definitively denying them the chance to reform."

- In the amended version, the reference made in the earlier version to legitimating the death penalty "in cases of extreme gravity" is omitted.

- Cases of "absolute necessity" for the death penalty "are now very rare, if not in practice non-existent." In other words, the death penalty is now considered to be virtually unnecessary "as a result of steady improvements in the organization of the penal system."

- Although the penalty should be "commensurate with the gravity of the crime" and punishment should be "adequate," it should be "applied in a very limited way" so as to offer to the offender "an incentive and help to change his or her behavior and be rehabilitated." The emphasis is not on death but rather on a possible and desirable change in life.

- "Bloodless" means (i.e., means that do not result in death) should be used if sufficient because such means are more in keeping with two of the central features of Catholic social teaching, viz., the common good and the dignity of the human person.

This, then, is the official teaching of the Catholic Church today. The death penalty is not recommended, desirable, or an accepted form of punishment for crimes. The Catholic Church no longer finds adequate or convincing the arguments which have been put forward in the past for capital punishment. Although the state does, indeed, have the right to protect its citizens and to punish criminals, this does not in itself mean that capital punishment is necessarily warranted. There remains a strong presumption against capital punishment because taking the life of a person violates the most fundamental ethical norm of respecting life. In other words, the death penalty is not necessary in order to protect society, and criminals can be punished in a manner that does not destroy life.

Three Key Principles of Catholic Teaching

The Catholic Church's position can be seen to focus on three key principles, namely, the sanctity of human life, the possibility of moral conversion, and the common good.

- *The Sanctity of Human Life.* God is the Author and Lord of human life from conception to the grave and as such human life should be respected at all times. The value of human life is such that it is inalienable and cannot be forfeited except when another innocent life is being directly threatened. This is why the Church rejects suicide: not even the individual who possesses life is entitled to destroy that life. This belief even underlies and supports the natural right to life of a human being.
- *The Possibility of Moral Conversion.* The finality of death removes from a human being the possibility of repentance. Even the most hardened of criminals is still capable of change no matter how small that possibility may be. We can never know to what extent free will and moral awareness are no longer operative in any human being despite appearances. The grace of God can still work at the deepest level of what it is to be human and any change that is possible can only take place before death. As long as there is reasonable assurance that the criminal is no longer a threat to others, the opportunity for repentance should not be removed. While the crime is not excused, forgiveness of the criminal remains a core tenet of Christian belief. The Church's perspective is, of course, also influenced by its belief in the next life, a consideration that is not part of the legal penal code of justice.

- *The Common Good.* Central to the social teaching of the Catholic Church is the insistence that every human being is social by nature, a belief that is rooted in the Church's belief in the Blessed Trinity. Individual and community are essentially interrelated. Hence, we are responsible for one another. "Am I my brother's [and sister's] guardian?" (Genesis 4:10). The answer is: "Most definitely, yes." We are all products of our society and we are responsible for the kind of society we have produced. The common good demands that we take responsibility for the criminals in our society and do what we can to remove the conditions that aggravate criminal tendencies. Among these factors are poverty, racism, broken families, and lack of education. A society that is reduced to taking life as a means of respecting life has already begun to lose sight of the common bond which unites all human beings.

CONCERNS ABOUT THE DEATH PENALTY

Reasons against Capital Punishment

In addition to the three basic principles mentioned above, the following concerns are also raised against the death penalty:

- *The Danger of a Miscarriage of Justice.* Capital punishment can be unevenly and inequitably applied. The majority of those executed are poor, uneducated, and members of racial minorities. These people cannot afford the expert legal advice available to the wealthy and often are discriminated against by juries, which reflect the prejudices of a society or can be strongly influenced by public expectations. It is sometimes later demonstrated that those sentenced to death were innocent or were discriminated against in the sentencing process. However, the finality of capital punishment means that a miscarriage of justice cannot be corrected, nor can the executed later benefit from changes in the law or new evidence that could affect their conviction.

- *The Brutalizing Effect on Society.* Capital punishment is a gruesome practice that can harden and desensitize society, thus undermining respect and reverence for human life. Capital punishment demeans human life. Executing criminals is inhumane and contributes to a dangerous vindictive spirit in society. Indeed, even though carried out by the state, the death penalty is itself a form of violence which can have a brutalizing effect on society by perpetuating the cycle of violence. The need to satisfy what has been referred to as "a primal lust for vengeance" is surely not in the best interests of society. To calculate what the murderer "deserves" on this basis is to attempt to correct one form of violence with another. Executions only cheapen human life. Indeed, it has well been said, "Murder and capital punishment are not opposites that cancel one another but similars that breed their kind."[12]

  The existence of death row casts its dark shadow on all who are in contact with it. Wardens and guards are known to be deeply affected by it. Legal proceedings often involve excruciating delays before finally executing the criminal. Putting a murderer to death does not restore life to the murdered victim. The unnecessary taking of a human life does not correct the wrong of another human life taken.

- *The Existence of Alternative Means of Punishing.* A growing argument against capital punishment is that the need for punishment can be satisfied in other ways. There are alternatives to capital punishment such as life imprisonment without parole. Criminals, even murderers, still remain human beings and while they may lose the right to their freedom, they do not lose their right to life.

---

12 The statement is attributed to George Bernard Shaw.

Reasons in Favor of Capital Punishment

In striving toward the abolition of the death penalty, the Catholic Church is not unaware of the many legitimate concerns which are raised by some in favor of its retention. Among such concerns are:

- The need to appease the anger and emotional frustration of the victim's family, relations and friends as well as the indignation of society at large;
- The fear that the murderer may escape from prison or be released on parole;
- Scarcity of resources to cope with murderers in prison;
- The rehabilitation treatment, which may result in comfort rather than punishment to the murderer;
- The uselessness of murderers to society;
- The expense on taxpayers in keeping murderers alive in prison;
- The belief that murderers will never change.

These are all realistic anxieties which cannot be dismissed or ignored. In countries where the legal system is fragile and where prison security is weak, there is good reason for having reservations about removing the death penalty. However, despite these practical difficulties, the Catholic Church is more and more convinced that the value and dignity of human life is so precious and unique that none of these reasons can justify its unnecessary destruction.

CONCLUSION

Today, the Catholic Church has come to a clearer understanding of its position on capital punishment in the light of its interpretation of Scripture and the ongoing tradition of its social moral teaching.

The weight of the Church's teaching is against capital punishment, as indeed is the growing public opinion around the world reflected in the abolition of the death penalty in over a hundred countries. There has been a growing religious sensitivity and humanitarian consciousness that calls for the rejection of the state's right to take the life of anyone as a punishment for crimes such as murder, treason, rape, etc., no matter how heinous the crime may be.

The preservation of human life from conception to the moment of unavoidable death may well be seen by many as an ideal that cannot easily be implemented. Nonetheless, it is an ideal that the Catholic Church believes is not only worth striving for, but one which has numerous practical implications for the common good and for the manner in which human life is understood and treated.

10

EXPLORING THE ALTERNATIVE OF RESTORATIVE JUSTICE

MARK WOLFF, J.D., LL.M.
Professor of Law
Saint Thomas University School of Law, Miami Gardens, Florida

While not explicitly on the death penalty, this essay raises deeper questions about the very nature of our criminal justice system in the United States and asks about an alternative theory of justice that is emerging in many places around the world, namely, the theory of "restorative justice." In appendix 2, Professor Wolff provides an extended bibliography which serves as a valuable resource for future research on this important theme.

One need not investigate very deeply before concluding that the American criminal justice system is not working. As pointed out by John Braithwaite, "Few sets of institutional arrangements created in the West since the Industrial Revolution have been as large a failure as the criminal justice system."[1]

The American experience has been driven by the notion of retribution as a critical and indispensable element of the criminal justice system. Elected leaders have exploited the rhetoric of fear of crime

1 Braithwaite, John, "Restorative Justice and a Better Future," Dorothy J. Killam *Memorial Lecture*, Dalhousie University, 17 October 1996.

and criminals primarily for political and economic as opposed to social purposes.

What I will call the "American Culture of Incarceration" has created a building construction explosion for correctional facilities. During the 1980s and 1990s, the growing number of states that have adopted mandatory sentences, even for less serious offenses, has fueled a growing economy; the primary result is the caging in prisons of America's youth.[2] Probably not surprisingly, minorities and the lower socio-economic strata of American society disproportionately bear the brunt of increased imprisonment.[3]

Notwithstanding the foregoing, there has been little evaluation of the effectiveness or cost-benefit ratio of this growing trend. Because of the tremendous growth and the economic impact, the private sector has today become more involved in the criminal justice system, particularly in connection with the operation of correctional facilities.[4] The introduction of profit motive into this new economy does not bode well for the future.

The Offender

The disparate treatment of offenders with similar crimes is also extremely troubling, particularly while so called "white collar" criminals either escape responsibility completely, or if incarcerated at all, are sent to facilities that more closely resemble a country club with golf,

---

2 Braithwaite, John, *Crime, Shame and Reintegration* (Cambridge: Cambridge University Press, 1989).

3 The United States Department of Justice reports that African-Americans have a 16.2% chance of going to prison during their lifetime compared to a 9.4% chance for Hispanics and a 2.5% chance for Caucasians.

4 According to United States Department of Justice statistics, there were over 1.3 million prisoners under Federal or State jurisdiction on December 31, 1998. State prisons were operating at nearly 22% above capacity while Federal prisons were operating at 27% above capacity, further spurning the move towards privatization of correctional facilities.

tennis, and other recreational facilities.[5] Conversely, another criminal engaged in the theft of comparatively less in value may be sentenced to a prison where the orientation is a beating to be repeated regularly, and daily life involves being raped and the possibility of contracting AIDS.[6] The dehumanization of the penal experience transforms the youthful property thief or drug offender into a hardened criminal destined to a life of escalating violence and crime.[7] Politicians climbing the political ladder of their own personal success are politically and economically wedded to this new and growing American Culture of Incarceration with its concomitant fundamental retributive focus.

THE VICTIM

The American public seems soothed and placated by the notion that the victims' right to retribution has been satisfied; the guilty have been punished and the injured party vindicated. This is simply not true. In our criminal justice system, the victim is disconnected from the offender and the process.[8]

First, the police stigmatize, humiliate and ostracize the offender, creating social outcasts unworthy of dignity and a place in the community. The offender is not required to accept responsibility for the acts committed, but rather is engaged in a game, initially with police authorities. From the offender's standpoint, the system is flawed and inconsistent, and the focus is not on the immorality of the act or the traumatic consequences suffered by the victim, but rather how to escape accountability by manipulating the system.

---

5 Zehr, Howard. *Changing Lenses: A New Focus for Criminal Justice* (Scottsdale, PA: Herald Press, 1990).

6 The U.S. Department of Justice reported that the number of HIV-positive prisoners grew by 34% from 1991 to 1997. Of all HIV-positive prison inmates, 26% were confirmed AIDS cases.

7 See Braithwaite, supra note 1.

8 Pettit, Philip and Braithwaite, John. *Not Just Deserts: A Republican Theory of Criminal Justice* (Oxford: Oxford University Press, 1990).

If the police is able to make a prima facie case, round two of the game continues with professional prosecutors and defense lawyers. The rules of the game are complicated and perversely inconsistent – only understood, if at all, by the lawyers and judges. If the crime is one involving personal face-to-face violence or theft, the victim may be allowed to play the role of a well-coached witness. The defense lawyer will assure that the experience will not prove to be cathartic and healing, but adversarial. Otherwise the victim is a mere faceless bystander whose frustration and anger is required to ferment outside the system.

The criminal forced into the game is not concerned about the moral wrong to the victim or society, but is engaged in a disconnected process looking for a Get-out-of-Jail-Free card. The victim, also isolated and disconnected from the process, becomes focused on revenge, and the unnatural nature of the process consequently represses the true traumatic human emotions associated with the status of victim.[9]

If the offender is convicted, the guilt, humiliation, shame, isolation, and stigmatization provide the status of an untouchable – an evil person relegated to association in a prison criminal subculture.

SOCIETY

Some will conclude that society has been served and justice has been done. The statistics of recidivism, however, refute unquestionably any such conclusion.[10] Prison is used to brutalize the weak and educate the imprisoned with new skills to be employed in the criminal labor market upon release.

---

9 Scheff, Tom and Retzinger, Suzanne. Emotions and Violence: Shame and Rage in Destructive Conflicts (Lexington Books, 1991).

10 The U.S. Department of Justice reported that of the 105,580 persons released form prisons in 11 States in 1983, an estimated 62.5% were rearrested for a felony or serious misdemeanor within 3 years of their release.

This bleak picture of the criminal justice system is not overly harsh but generously sketchy. Our criminal justice system is fatally flawed, and we must examine alternatives or be destined to live as prisoners of our own failed vengeance. One such alternative, Restorative Justice, began to take root in the 1970s, but its traditions are well established in the teaching of Jesus and ancient tribal cultures.[11]

RESTORATIVE JUSTICE

Restorative justice focuses not only upon the victim's needs but also upon the offender, and at the grass roots, the community.[12] It can be conceptualized as a community-centered criminal justice system. At the heart of Restorative Justice is not only restoring the victim but the restoration of offenders and the community. The concept is to restore not only the victim's property or injury, but through professionally facilitated encounters between victim and offender, the victim's sense of dignity and security, thus restoring a sense of empowerment,[13] deliberative democracy, social support from family and friends, and the abiding feeling that justice has been served.[14]

The offender also needs restoration from the shame and stigmatization associated with commission of a crime and arrest. In the dialogue process, it may become apparent that the community must share responsibility with the offender who now shoulders the indignity and humiliation. The restoration of dignity is a by-product of the process through which the offender accepts responsibility for the

---

11 Zehr. Howard. "Retributive Justice, Restorative Justice," New Perspectives on Crime and Justice: Occasional Papers of the MCC Canada Victim Offender Ministries Program and the MCC US Office of Criminal Justice, Issue 4, September 1985.

12 See Braithwaite *supra note* 1.

13 Christie, Nils. "Conflicts as Property," *British Journal of Criminology* 17:1-15, 1978.

14 Tyler, Tom. *Why People Obey the Law* (New Haven: Yale University Press, 1990).

evil of the act without labeling the actor as evil and worthless. The offender must confront the shame, accept responsibility for the victim's loss, and feel obligation to apologize to complete the process. The genuineness and integrity of the process are critical to restoring the offender.

The community is also the beneficiary of the restorative justice process if it similarly accepts its responsibility for the social and economic circumstances which may have directly caused or contributed to the actions of the offender. The community development is conditioned by the process, and initiatives can be taken through civic, governmental, charitable, and religious organizations to ameliorate the community's responsibility. The process both sensitizes the community and challenges it to respond with creative solutions to the root problem rather than myopically focus on retribution. In this regard, restorative justice forces the community to address larger social issues such as poverty, hunger, unemployment, homelessness, discrimination and racism.

Restorative justice, then, is centered in a dialogue between not only the victim and offender, but also the local community at the micro level and ultimately society at the macro level.[15] Restorative justice has been successfully adopted for juvenile and young adult offenders in connection with property, and the so-called victimless crimes of drugs and prostitution.[16]

The restorative model diverts the offender out of the criminal justice system, decriminalizing the process. Prisons are replaced with habilitation or wellness centers that are not penal and dehumanizing. Through counseling and group interaction, offenders deal with their rudimentary causal problems such as aggression, drug or alcohol

---

15 Morrell, V. "Restorative Justice: An Overview," *Criminal Justice Quarterly* 5:3-7, 1993.

16 Morris, Allison and Maxwell, Gabrielle. "Juvenile Justice in New Zealand: A New Paradigm," *Australian and New Zealand Journal of Criminology 26*: 72-90, 1992.

abuse, and sexual deviancy so they may be restored to respect as members of the community.[17]

Mediation with professional facilitators and/or community panels replaces the adversarial criminal justice trial system, where professional prosecutors and defense attorneys play by a technical set of rules with their own language of legalese. The disconnect between victim and offender, act and actor, actor and moral responsibility, victim and feelings of disempowerment, and offender and shame in the retributive criminal justice system is reconnected with all in restorative dialogue.

Restorative Cultural Traditions

The Western criminal justice system with individual guilt, alienation, and retribution at its core is not the only model; rather, most ancient cultures had well functioning restorative traditions.[18]

We as Catholics need only glance at the New Testament for the words of Jesus. The importance of the dignity of each human person is required by the fact that we are all brothers and sisters of one Lord. It is this ultimate truth that necessitates we treat each other with love, respect, and kindness. We understand and condemn the evil of the morally wrong act but may not vilify the offending person, a creature of God and temple of the Holy Spirit. "Blessed are the peacemakers: for they shall be called the children of God."[19] As Catholic Christians, we have been charged to "Do unto others as you would have them do unto you." Jesus did not teach revenge and punishment, but mercy and forgiveness.

---

17 See Braithwaite *supra note* 1.

18 Melton, A.P. "Indigenous Justice Systems and Tribal Society," *Judicature* 79(3): 12 & 33, 1995.

19 Matthew 5:1-12.

11

FORMING A DIALOGUE GROUP TO STUDY THE QUESTION

SALLIE LATKOVICH, C.S.J., D.MIN.
Assistant Professor
Blessed Edmund Rice School for Pastoral Ministry
Arcadia, Florida

The "Right to Life" movement is alive and well in the Roman Catholic Church – regarding the rights of the unborn and fierce opposition to abortion. By contrast, however, there is relatively little grass roots support for and even less active commitment to opposing the death penalty as practiced by the criminal justice system.

One might observe that there is not indifference to capital punishment on the grass roots level, but actual support for it. Let me provide two examples:

The first example is a letter to the editor published in the Feb. 10, 2000 issue of *The Florida Catholic.* It was written in response to the Florida Catholic bishops' letter on the death penalty:

> *I am a firm believer in the death penalty. I was a POW in World War II. Our local newspaper had an article on the murder of a 28-year-old, mother of two, a waitress who was murdered by strangulation on her way to work. Do any of our bishops think that killer does not deserve the death penalty by electrocution or injection? (William J. Flynn, Miami)*

The second example was an excellent segment of the television program entitled "The West Wing." The story line of this segment focused on the execution of a man who had killed a police officer; thus, the criminal's execution was a federal offense. The program highlighted the excruciating choice faced by the president of the United States to allow the execution to occur, or to grant a stay of execution and/or pardon.

Strikingly, the writers of this segment had one of the president's advisors seeking spiritual advice from his rabbi. The rabbi encouraged a decision favoring life and not death. Furthermore, the president, a Catholic himself, has a heart-to-heart conversation with a priest-friend, during which the president receives a written memo that the execution has been carried out. The closing scene of the segment is the president beginning his confession.

Why didn't the president act on his personal moral conviction or that of his Jewish advisor? Because the popular opinion was in favor of capital punishment.

As I make additions to the original paper, there is yet another that provides more indication of popular opinion. It is the tragic Oklahoma City bombing, for which Timothy McVeigh was publicly executed. Although there were individuals (who lost loved ones in the bombing) who publicly spoke against the death penalty, it is safe to say that pubic opinion fell clearly on the side of capital punishment. In the Oklahoma City bombing, there was wide use of the word "justice" in the aftermath. It has been used synonymously with "retaliation." The biblical understanding of justice could not be further from either situation. This will be discussed later in this proposal.

The hierarchy, the *magisterium* of our Church, has spoken strongly and publicly against capital punishment. As a Church, we might carry on a debate with the writer of the above letter, or with the populace of the United States referred to in the television program. Or we may in fact debate with those who cheered at the execution of Timothy McVeigh. We might seek to change their minds on the death penalty by calling for obedience to the authority of the Church or by rational argument.

My proposed pastoral response in this paper, however, is to seek to change people's hearts, not minds. Hopefully, their minds and votes will follow.

How do we set about changing people's hearts?

I propose to offer three key movements. In addition, these suggestions might best be carried out in the context of dialogue groups in basic community settings within the diocese and/or the parish, or in a high school religion class, or on a college campus. Let me first describe the movements, and then give practical suggestions for forming and facilitating these movements in dialogue groups.

THREE KEY MOVEMENTS

- *Tending to People's Experiences and Feelings.* The first movement I suggest in facilitating a change of heart is to tend to people's life experiences and feelings. Dianne Bergant, a leading scholar in the Hebrew Scriptures who teaches at the Catholic Theological Union in Chicago, makes this observation: "Some say that experience is a good teacher. I say that experience is the only teacher." Thus, we must tend to people's feelings of victimization and loss, as well as the supposed relief of retribution.
- *Shifting Feelings toward Justice.* The second movement in a change of heart is to facilitate a shift of feeling on the axis of justice. This entails a clarification of the meaning of justice and what justice demands, according to God's Word in the Scriptures. This clarification would show the gross misinterpretation of justice in its common usage, particularly when one speaks of the "criminal justice system." Clearly, this implies a clarion call to conversion.
- *Calling Forth Compassion.* The third and final movement in a change of heart is to call forth compassion, in the Gospel sense;

indeed to suggest forgiveness. This is a difficult task in a culture where litigation and extracting the proverbial "pound of flesh" has become the norm.

The Dialogue Group

The forum for these movements to take place would appropriately be in a diocesan or parish setting of a dialogue group. Another obvious place for a dialogue group is in an educational setting: for students in religious education or in Catholic elementary or high school, and certainly those on a college or university campus.

Such a group could be called together by a bishop or a pastor, a pastoral staff member, a social justice committee, a campus minister, or individuals who feel strongly opposed to capital punishment. A good convener/facilitator is very important; someone who is committed to this issue, and has good facilitation skills by personal gift or training.

The invitation to such a group might be by way of challenge, a "dare" of sorts: to gather for the purpose of dialogue regarding this important issue in our world and Church.

A good number of people to gather for such a group would be between eight and twelve. This would allow for real dialogue, in an atmosphere where trust can be established. In the parishes where this proposal was piloted, it seemed that the first gatherings were with like-minded individuals. This is a good thing. Then, those who are in opposition to the death penalty gain confidence by sharing their views in a guided dialogue with others.

After participating in the process with "kindred spirits," individuals may feel more able to lead the dialogue process with others who are not like-minded on the death penalty issue. Note that the proposed process is quite different from "talking them into it." Rather, it might be described as evoking the truth in others' life experiences, in light of the Gospel.

In gathering such a group for dialogue, it would be best to evoke a commitment from the participants to come to all three sessions, since the trust level that grows is important.

It is unlikely that each of the three movements would be accomplished in one sitting apiece; however, it would be a significant beginning to plan on three meetings. Each meeting should have a published start and finish time, which are adhered to. If further meetings are desired, the group can then discern and plan the steps to follow.

One additional suggestion is that the "place" of meeting for this dialogue group be either at a round table or with chairs arranged in a circle. It is important that every member of the group be able to see and hear every other member in the group. The ambience of a candle and open Scripture in the center of the group makes an important symbolic statement of seeking enlightenment, the light of Christ, in God's Word.

Tending to Peoples' Feelings of Victimization and Loss of Control

Unfortunately, and indeed sadly, most people learn or are enculturated to the following similar theories of life which affirm each other even as they come from three different disciplines:

First, we learn from the Hebrew Scriptures that one has the right to demand "an eye for an eye, a tooth for a tooth." (Exodus 21:24) Carrying on that statement, those in favor of the death penalty say: "a life for a life." Secondly, a fundamental theory of physics is one of Newton's basic principles of motion, which states that every action has an equal and opposite reaction. Thus, the equal reaction to the taking of a life is the taking of a life, according to those proponents of the death penalty. And finally, in literature, Shakespeare underscores the ethic of demanding a "pound of flesh" in payment of any debt that is unpaid or unable to be paid. The "debt" of death, then, is to be repaid by the flesh of another.

These learnings may be unconscious, but I propose that they are rather deeply held feelings in our culture, where victimization and loss of control demand the response to which we have been encultured. The death penalty is not primarily a logically determined punishment, but a more deeply engrained feeling/need for retribution. Its "appropriateness" may be argued by the lessons above from Scripture, science, and literature.

If indeed the practice of capital punishment is primarily emotional and not rational, the first movement in the effort to change hearts must be to tend to people's feelings, particularly of victimization and loss of control.

Road rage has become an often-reported occurrence, along with editorials about the issue. This is a clear example of people's anger erupting into rage when they feel they have been wronged by another driver. In the case of road rage, anger is the primary response to a wrong that has been done, and the theories listed above become reality. Road rage is but one example of a number of societal situations where a person may feel victim. The resultant anger festers until it can be expressed and dealt with. There are countless other examples that might be cited here.

A person whose life has been taken by another is an obvious victim of a crime, but others profoundly affected by the loss of that life are also victims. It is these people who are left to live with their anger. The above-mentioned theories from Scripture, science, and literature point to retribution as the appropriate outlet for the resultant anger of victimization. Thus, the first effort in changing people's hearts is simply to tend to anger.

So, at the first meeting of a dialogue group focusing on capital punishment, here is a possible agenda:

1. *Opening Prayer.* The sole purpose of gathering the group in God, and highlighting God's mercy.

2. *Introductions.* Each individual is asked to share his or her name, background, why they have come and what they hope for. The purpose here is to build trust.

3. *Brief Presentation by facilitator* on the dynamic of victimization and its resultant anger. The facilitator might share a true story from his or her own life about having been victimized.[1]

4. *Invitation* to members of the group to share their own experiences of being victims, and the anger which results. (Or, if the video were used, commentary on the stories told, with addition of personal stories of those in the group.)

5. *Conversation.* The facilitator might begin a conversation about how we tend – both appropriately and inappropriately – to deal with anger.

6. *Conclusion.* The facilitator might mention the ways we have been taught/enculturated to respond, as listed above . . . and suggest that God's Word has a different message. That is the invitation to return for the second dialogue: What indeed is justice?

WHAT, INDEED, IS JUSTICE?

Here again, we have been wrongly enculturated to presume that justice has to do with fairness and equality at best, or the legal winning of a civil case at worst. Picking up on the conversation above regarding retribution, some may even claim that retribution for an evil done is just. As mentioned in the introduction, this has certainly been the primary use of the word "justice" in relation to the death penalty.

---

1 There is an excellent video available that highlights this dynamic in the life experiences of real folks. The video is entitled *Healing the Heart, Forgive and Remember.* It is available from Films for the Humanities & Sciences at 1-800-257-5126.

One seldom hears a homily preached about the meaning of justice, or given concrete examples of acting justly. A simple definition of justice, found clearly in the Hebrew Scriptures, is: *the quality of acting in right relationship with one another, in covenant with God.* A good, readable resource as background study is *Social Justice in the Hebrew Bible* by Bruce V. Malchow.[2]

I often try to illustrate the above definition by sharing this true story. There is a family I know where loving parents have three sons. The first two sons are "typical, normal" boys. The third son, however, is a child with Down Syndrome. The parents have gone to great lengths to provide services for their special child. One day, the mother confessed that she felt guilty about the time, attention, and resources that their youngest son had received; and the older two had not. (The older two were well cared for.) The mother said: "It doesn't seem fair." I responded, "Maybe not, but it is clearly just." The youngest of the three sons, with Down Syndrome, was in greater need, and simply received what he needed.

That's a nice story, you say, but what does it have to do with JUSTICE, and particularly with capital punishment?

I propose that we as a Church must facilitate the conversion in people's hearts to justice!

In other words, what does it mean to be in a "right relationship" with a person who has committed murder? How can we best protect society AND care for this person in the most humane way?

The Hebrew word for justice or righteousness found in the Scriptures is *sedaqah*, from the root *sdq*. A study of the uses of *sdq* reveals that it refers to a relationship between two parties and implies behavior which fulfills the claims arising from such an involvement. *Sdq* is,

---

2 A Michael Glazier Book of The Liturgical Press, 1996

thus, the fulfillment of the demands of a relationship with God or a person.[3]

It is a strange relationship between a victim and a perpetrator; but nevertheless, a relationship exists. In light of the Scriptural understanding and practice of justice, the death penalty is never a just conclusion to the relationship.

It is important to include the notion of what has come to be titled: "Restorative Justice." Again, striving for "right relationship," restorative justice deals with the needs of the victim, the ones left feeling victimized by a particular crime. The offender is indeed to be held accountable, but not by death. And, restorative justice does enable the affected community to take part in this process.

For some, opposition to the death penalty seems to minimize the needs of the victims. In justice, the victims' needs must be addressed. Among these needs might be:

1. A forum where they can ask: "Why me?" "What did I do to deserve this?" "Why my child?"
2. Where there is recognition of the wrong done, by the community and by the offender.
3. Assurance of safety, and reassurance that the crime will not be repeated.
4. An apology made to the families of victims.
5. Coming to meaning or significance, where one's pain has positive impact on the world. (An example would be Mothers Against Drunk Driving; or membership with Compassionate Friends, a group of parents who have lost children to death.)

How might hearts be changed to an understanding of justice that reverences life, even in pronouncing a judgment on someone who

---

3 Bruce V. Malchow, *Social Justice in the Hebrew Bible* (Collegeville, MN: The Liturgical Press, 1996), p.16.

has done death? Once again, for a dialogue group, here is a proposed agenda for a second such meeting:

1. *Opening prayer.* Again gathering the group in God and God's own quality of justice.

2. *Re-introductions.* Even if this is a second gathering; establishing a group of friends, and not strangers; and calling forth at least a shared faith in God (even if disagreement still exists regarding capital punishment).

3. *Brief Presentation* by the facilitator about the quality of justice. It is important to clarify the distinction between our cultural understanding of justice as fairness, or again as retribution; and the Scriptural understanding of being in right relationship with God and one another (see resource mentioned above).

4. *Caveat.* It is important for the facilitator NOT to receive individual understandings of justice, but rather their RESPONSES to the presentation they have just heard.

5. *Conclusion.* Rather than concluding the dialogue with hope for agreement, perhaps the dialogue will end simply with hope for conversion to the justice to which we are called by God.

Calling Forth Compassion, Indeed Forgiveness

Among the three movements I have proposed, this third one is undoubtedly the most difficult. We, in our culture, are not taught to forgive, are not shown forgiveness in the media, do not know how to begin to let go of anger or rage, to choose to act justly, to extend compassion by forgiveness.

Some years ago, an Ursuline Sister of Cleveland was found brutally murdered in a wooded area of the Motherhouse property. Once her body was discovered, a trail in the snow led directly to the killer. The Ursuline Sisters publicly asked for mercy for the man. The people of Cleveland responded in disbelief and anger that the Sisters would forgive one who committed such a crime. This is also a good example of how individuals' feelings of victimization rise up in the public arena. It was a powerful moment, and a powerful model.

This true story only highlights the "state of heart" of our culture, which is still in favor of the death penalty, and indeed startled by the call to forgive. It is no wonder, for we hold some misconceptions about forgiveness that are stumbling blocks for us. Perhaps recognizing the blocks on the way is the first step to making our way to forgiveness.

In her little book entitled *Seventy Times Seven*, Doris Donnelly outlines several misconceptions about forgiveness. These are:

- *Misconception 1*: Forgiveness is easy . . . the fact is that forgiveness involves a process that doesn't come naturally.
- *Misconception 2*: Forgiveness can't be rushed ... we owe it to each other to offer time to confront our wounds, to face our hurts head-on, to vent our emotions. Only then can real healing begin.
- *Misconception 3:* Forgiveness means forgetting . . . most of the time, we don't forget and aren't expected to. Memories exert power in our conscious and unconscious lives; but the power of the painful memory will decrease once forgiven.
- *Misconception 4:* Forgiveness is a weakness . . . hate and revenge never put us in control; they do just the opposite. They put us in bondage to someone else's evil deeds by counting our bitter reactions to them. Forgiveness is indeed a strength that sets us free.
- *Misconception 5:* The only one who benefits from forgiveness is the one who is forgiven . . . it really is the freedom – for the forgiver – that is at stake here. Without forgiveness, both the doer of the evil and the sufferer are enclosed in a vicious cycle of

> vengeance capable of mutilating, if not destroying, each of them.[4]

It is obvious that these misconceptions must be countered with the truth. The truth is that forgiveness is always the beginning of a new life, which is exactly what is needed and sought after the experience of death.

Still again, it is evident that the movement to forgiveness is not merely a rational lesson-plan; it is a nurturing of belief in a God who forgives, and invites us to do the same. How might this be addressed? We return to our dialogue group:

1. *Opening prayer.* The purpose of gathering the group in God; may involve simply listening to several of the Gospel passages, which teach or model forgiveness. These might be read by different members of the group, with a short time of silence in between each reading. Some of the suggested passages are:
   - Matthew 18:21-22: How often must I forgive?
   - John 20:20: Peace be with you…
   - Matthew 5:23-25: Go and be reconciled…
   - John 13:15: I have given you example…
   - Luke 23:34: God, forgive them…
   - Luke 6:36: Be compassionate…
   - John 8:11: Neither do I condemn you…
   - Matthew 18:33: Were you not bound, then, to have pity on your fellow servant?
2. *Introductions.* Again to establish a gathering of friends and not strangers.

---

4 Doris Donnelly, *Seventy Time Seven* (Erie, PA: Pax Christi USA, 1993), p. 31.

3. Participants may be invited to describe feelings when they had sought revenge for an injustice done to them; and, again, feelings when they had desired to forgive.

4. Conversation/dialogue about the differences in feelings.

5. Facilitator might raise the question of where one draws the strength and support to forgive. How might forgiveness be expressed, shown, realized? (Note: Another fine video recommendation is *Healing the Soul: Religious Perspectives on Forgiveness.*[5])

6. Again, at the conclusion of this third session of the dialogue group, the group may desire to continue. If so, the group might discern a plan for doing so.

In conclusion, the primary proposal of this paper is that, to end capital punishment, we must facilitate the changing of people's hearts, trusting that their minds and votes will follow.

I specifically suggest that this change of heart might occur in three necessary steps:

- *tending to people's life experiences and feelings;*
- *facilitating the shift of feeling on the axis of justice;*
- *calling forth feelings of compassion and forgiveness.*

These three movements will best be addressed not in a large assembly, but in small dialogue groups, in gatherings of friends on the diocesan or parish level, or in an educational setting.

History shows us that significant social change has occurred from the grass-roots up, and not vice versa. The dialogue group is the soil where seeds of justice and forgiveness will take root and grow to

---

5 Available from Films for the Humanities & Sciences at 1-800-257-5126. The video would be a fine source of discussion and dialogue; a little "safer" way to get at the issue of FORGIVENESS without putting group members "on the spot."

societal proportions. What better model do we have in this regard than Jesus, along with the dialogue group that became the Church?

APPENDICES

APPENDIX 1

CATHOLIC-ORIENTED RESOURCES ON THE DEATH PENALTY

FRANK MCNEIRNEY
National Coordinator
Catholics Against Capital Punishment, Bethesda, Maryland

The following is a list of publications, visual materials, and organizational websites considered to be of special interest to Catholic individuals and groups involved in activities relating to the death penalty. Please note that this list includes only those resources that are specifically Catholic-oriented, and that space limitations preclude the addition of hundreds of others (national, international, state, religious and secular) that may be of value. A comprehensive list of all such resources can be found on the website of the Washington, DC-based Death Penalty Information Center, at <www.deathpenaltyinfo.org> (go to "Resources," then click on "Related Sites").

- Beaumont (Texas), Diocese of. Our Faith, OUR CASE AGAINST THE DEATH PENALTY [Video, 10 min.]. *Includes footage filmed inside the Texas death row and features comments by Dead Man Walking author Sr. Helen Prejean, C.S.J., Beaumont Bishop Curtis J. Guillory, S.V.D., and Deacon Al O'Brien, director of the diocese's Office of Criminal Justice Ministry. Includes an 8-page study guide. Available from Office of Criminal Justice Ministry, PO Box 3948, Beaumont TX 77704-3948.*

- Bernardin, Joseph Cardinal. CONSISTENT ETHIC OF LIFE. *Chicago: Sheed and Ward, 1988. ISBN 1556121202.*
- Bosco, Antoinette. CHOOSING MERCY: A MOTHER OF MURDER VICTIMS PLEADS TO END THE DEATH PENALTY. *Maryknoll, NY: Orbis Books, 2001. 240 pp. ISBN: 57075-358-X. Catholic journalist discusses her feelings following the murder of her son and his wife.*
- Brooklyn (NY), Diocese of, Sanctity of Life Commission. MERCY AND JUSTICE: THE MORALITY OF THE DEATH PENALTY [Video, 18 min.]. *Features footage of Pope John Paul II's Jan. 1999 address in St. Louis, in which he called capital punishment "both cruel and unnecessary," plus comments by three anti-death penalty parents whose children were murdered. Includes a discussion guide and a copy of Bishop Thomas V. Daily's 1999 pastoral letter on the issue. Available from Public Information Office, Diocese of Brooklyn, PO Box C, Brooklyn NY 11202.*
- Brugger, E. Christian, CAPITAL PUNISHMENT AND ROMAN CATHOLIC TRADITION. *University of Notre Dame Press, 2003. 296 pp. ISBN: 026802359X*
- Hodgkins, Peter, and William A. Schabas, eds. CAPITAL PUNISHMENT: STRATEGIES FOR ABOLITION. *Cambridge University Press, 2004. 388 pp. ISBN: 052185908. Chapter 5, by James Megivern, discusses the topic of* Religion *and the Death Penalty in the United States of America: Past and Present.*
- Cabana, Donald A. DEATH AT MIDNIGHT: THE CONFESSIONS OF AN EXECUTIONER. *Boston: Northeastern University Press, 1996. 200 pp. ISBN: 1555533566. Catholic prison official recounts how his experiences as warden of Mississippi's death row led to his change of heart about the death penalty.*
- California Catholic Conference. THE GOSPEL OF LIFE AND CAPITAL PUNISHMENT: A REFLECTION PIECE AND STUDY

- GUIDE, JULY 1999. *http://www.cacatholic.org/h/bs/bs91109-83267.html*

- CATECHISM OF THE CATHOLIC CHURCH, 2ND EDITION. *Washington, DC: U.S. Conference of Catholic Bishops, 1997. [Article 5 (Sections 2265-2267) contains material relating to Church teaching on the death penalty.] http://www.usccb.org/catechism/text/index.htm*

- *Catholic Common Ground Initiative.* THE DEATH PENALTY [Video, 28 min.]. *Explores how the Church's stance on the death penalty issue compares to, and fits with, its teachings on abortion and assisted suicide. Featured are comments by Georgetown University's Rev. John Langan, S.J., Virginia legislator Robert McDonnell, Catholic U. of America dean Jude P. Dougherty, and Bud Welch of Murder Victims' Families for Reconciliation. Available from CCG Initiative, National Pastoral Life Center, 18 Bleecker St., New York, NY 10012-2404.*

- CATHOLICS AGAINST CAPITAL PUNISHMENT (CACP) [Website]. *http://www.cacp.org. Contains news of Catholic-oriented efforts to end the death penalty; text of the current edition of CACP News Notes; links to papal and ecclesiastical statements on the issue; FAQs about the Catholic Church's stance on capital punishment; and excerpts from Vatican documents and the Catholic Catechism.*

- Catholics Against Capital Punishment. CACP NEWS NOTES. *Newsletter about developments in Catholic Church teachings and diocesan- and parish-based programs relating to the death penalty. Available from CACP, PO Box 5706, Bethesda MD 20824-5706. Can also be downloaded from http://www.cacp.org*

- Colorado Catholic Conference. TURNING AWAY FROM VIOLENCE: AN APPEAL BY THE BISHOPS OF COLORADO TO END THE DEATH PENALTY, May 10, 2001. *http://www.archden.org/archbishop/docs/death_penalty_bishops.htm*

- Comiskey, Paul W. CREATING AND PUBLICIZING AN ANTI-DEATH PENALTY RESOLUTION FOR YOUR PARISH. *2000; up-*

dated edition scheduled for Fall 2003. 50 pp. Privately printed; available from Paul W. Comiskey, 900 G St. (#302), Sacramento, CA 95814.

- DEAD MAN WALKING [motion picture]. *Screenplay by Tim Robbins. Gramercy Pictures,1995. 122 min. Adaptation of Sr. Helen Prejean's book of the same name.*

- DEAD MAN WALKING STUDY PACKET. *Philadelphia: American Friends Service Committee, Religious Organizing Against the Death Penalty Project. 12 pp. Booklet designed for use with group viewings of Dead Man Walking motion picture. Examines capital punishment from a faith-based perspective. Includes guidelines for facilitators, discussion questions, facts about the death penalty, and suggestions for further action. Available from AFSC, 1501 Cherry St., Philadelphia PA 19102, or through http://www.deathpenaltyreligious.org/resources.html*

- DECLARATION OF LIFE. *A legal document designed to be notarized when signed, in which an individual signifies that if he or she is ever a victim of a homicide, he/she does not want the murderer to be executed. Developed by the Sisters of Mercy Brooklyn Regional Community. Can be downloaded from http://www.brooklynmercy.org/cherishlifecircle.html*

- Dulles, Avery Cardinal, S.J. REMARKS ON FAITH TRADITIONS AND THE DEATH PENALTY, *presentation given at "A Call for Reckoning: Religion and the Death Penalty," a conference sponsored by the Pew Forum on Religion and Public Life, Jan. 25, 2002 at the University of Chicago. (Conference Proceedings also include texts of presentations by Associate U.S. Supreme Court Justice Antonin Scalia, Oklahoma Gov. Frank Keating, and Notre Dame Law School Prof. Richard Garnett.) http://pewforum.org/deathpenalty/resources*

- Elder, Joy. LETHAL JUSTICE: ONE MAN'S JOURNEY OF HOPE ON DEATH ROW. *Hyde Park, NY: New City Press, 2002. 168 pp. ISBN: 1-56548-164-X. $12.95. Welsh Catholic nun describes her correspondence and visits with a prisoner who was executed after 12 years on Texas's death row.*

- Fiorenza, Joseph A. STATEMENT OF THE U.S. CONFERENCE OF CATHOLIC BISHOPS' PRESIDENT ON THE EXECUTION OF TIMOTHY MCVEIGH, JUNE 11, 2001. *http://www.usccb.org/comm/archives/2001/01-104.htm*

- Florida Catholic Conference. TALKING ABOUT THE DEATH PENALTY [Video, 13 min.]. *Available in both English and Spanish and featuring introductions by the state's bishops, this video seeks to provide, in the words of FCC executive director Mike McCarron, "an opportunity for Catholics and others to come together and talk" about the issue. Can be viewed on the Conference's website, and there are no restrictions on parish groups or schools making copies.* *http://www.flacathconf.org/Issuesinfo/Capitalpunishmenttable.htm*

- Florida Catholic Conference. CATHOLIC CHURCH TEACHING ON THE DEATH PENALTY (text of June 2002 brochure). *http://www.flacathconf.org/Publications/Brochure/DPcardbr02.htm*

- FOR WHOM THE BELLS TOLL [Website]. *http://www.curenational.org/~bells. A national initiative encouraging Catholic parishes and other religious organizations to toll their bells whenever an execution takes place. A 6-page informational brochure about the initiative is available from Sr. Dorothy Briggs, O.P., 12 Ricker Rd., Newton, MA 02458.*

- George, Francis Cardinal, O.M.I. LENTEN STATEMENT ON DEATH PENALTY MORATORIUM, APRIL 19, 2000. http://www.archchicago.org/cardinal/statement/stats_00/stat_041900b.shtm

- Gracida, Rene H. CAPITAL PUNISHMENT AND THE SACREDNESS OF LIFE. *In: Shepherds Speak: American Bishops Confront the Social and Moral Issues that Challenge Christians Today, ed. by D. M. Corrado and J. F. Hinchey. New York: Crossroad/Herder and Herder, 1986.*

- Hehir, J. Bryan. CONSISTENT ETHIC OF LIFE. *In: The HarperCollins Encyclopedia of Catholicism, ed. by Richard P. McBrien. San Francisco: HarperSanFrancisco, 1995. ISBN: 0060653388.*
- Holy See, The, Secretariat of State. DECLARATION OF THE HOLY SEE TO THE FIRST WORLD CONGRESS ON THE DEATH PENALTY, JUNE 21, 2001, *in Strasbourg, France, presented by Msgr. Paul Gallagher, special envoy to the Council of Europe. http://www.vatican.va/roman_curia/secretariat_state/documents/rc_seg-st_doc_20010621_death-penalty_en.html*
- Hopcke, Robert H. SIX SIMPLE THINGS CATHOLICS CAN DO TO END THE DEATH PENALTY. *2002. 4 pp. A reprint from the May 24, 2002 issue of CACP News Notes. Available from Catholics against Capital Punishment, PO Box 5706, Bethesda MD 20824-5706. [More extensive version planned for forthcoming publication in book form.]*
- Indiana Catholic Conference. TALKING ABOUT THE DEATH PENALTY [Video, 10 min.]. *This video "gently but clearly presents capital punishment for what it is – the taking of human life," says Lafayette (Ind.) Bishop William L. Higi. Featured are comments by Notre Dame U. law professor Charles Rice, the state's bishops, and others. Available from the Office of Family Life, Diocese of Fort Wayne-South Bend, 114 W. Wayne St., South Bend IN 46601.*
- Indiana Catholic Conference. TALKING ABOUT THE DEATH PENALTY: FACTS AND CONSIDERATIONS. *http://www.indianacc.org/tables/death.html*
- John Paul II, Pope, et al. EXCERPTS FROM STATEMENTS BY POPE JOHN PAUL II ON THE DEATH PENALTY / EXCERPTS FROM OTHER VATICAN STATEMENTS ON THE DEATH PENALTY / CATECHISM OF THE CATHOLIC CHURCH LANGUAGE ON THE DEATH PENALTY. *2003. 6 pp. Available from Catholics against Capital Punishment, PO Box 5706, Bethesda, MD 20824-5706.*

- John Paul II, Pope. STATEMENTS BY THE HOLY FATHER ON THE DEATH PENALTY. *Contains excerpts from Jan. 25, 1999 Apostolic Exhortation Ecclesia in America; Jan. 27, 1999 homily at Papal Mass in St. Louis, MO; Dec. 25, 1998 Christmas Message; and death penalty-related passages from encyclical Evangelium Vitae (The Gospel of Life), 1995.* *http://www.usccb.org/sdwp/national/criminal/stlouissmt.htm*

- John Paul II, Pope. EVANGELIUM VITAE (THE GOSPEL OF LIFE). *1995, 196 pp. Publication 316-7 (English) and 317-5 (Spanish), available from the U.S. Conference of Catholic Bishops, 3211 4th St. N.E., Washington, DC 20017. Can also be downloaded from www.usccb.org/prolife/tdocs/evangel/evangeli.htm*

- Judd, Augustine, O.P. CATHOLICS AND CAPITAL PUNISHMENT: THE MORALITY OF CAPITAL PUNISHMENT ACCORDING TO CHURCH TEACHING. *New Haven, CT: Knights of Columbus Catholic Information Service. 28 pp. Publication 302, available from K. of C. Catholic Information Service, PO Box 1971, New Haven CT 06521-1971. Can also be downloaded from* *http://www.kofc.org/faith/cis/302/cp.cfm*

- Judd, Augustine, O.P. THE GOSPEL OF LIFE AND THE SENTENCE OF DEATH: CATHOLIC TEACHING ON CAPITAL PUNISHMENT. 2000. *In: 2000-2001 Respect Life Program of the U.S. Conference of Catholic Bishops' Secretariat for Pro-Life Activities.* *http://www.usccb.org/prolife/programs/rlp/00rljud.htm*

- Kentucky, Catholic Conference of. CAPITAL PUNISHMENT: THE DEATH OF MORALITY [Video, 12 min.]. *Targeted to middle and high school students, but also recommended as an introduction for adults interested in the topic. Discusses the issue from the viewpoints of both Catholic theology and pragmatic social policy, and is accompanied by a small-group study guide. Available from CCKY, 1042 Burlington Lane, Frankfort KY 40601.*

- Kramlich, Maureen. WE FORGIVE THOSE WHO TRESPASS AGAINST US. *2003. In: 2003-2004 Respect Life Program of the U.S. Conference of Catholic Bishops' Secretariat for Pro-Life Activities. http://www.usccb.org/prolife/programs/rlp/03rlkramlich.htm*

- Langan, John, S.J. CAPITAL PUNISHMENT. *In: The HarperCollins Encyclopedia of Catholicism, ed. by Richard P. McBrien. San Francisco: HarperSanFrancisco, 1995. ISBN: 0060653388.*

- Mahony, Roger Cardinal. A WITNESS TO LIFE: THE CATHOLIC CHURCH AND THE DEATH PENALTY. *May 25, 2000 address at the National Press Club, Washington, DC. http://www.usccb.org/sdwp/national/criminal/death/mahony1.htm*

- Martino, Renato R Cardinal. INTERVENTION BY H.E. ARCHBISHOP RENATO R. MARTINO, APOSTOLIC NUNCIO AND PERMANENT OBSERVER OF THE HOLY SEE TO THE UNITED NATIONS, BEFORE THE THIRD COMMITTEE OF THE 54TH SESSION OF THE GENERAL ASSEMBLY ON ITEM 116A, ABOLITION OF THE DEATH PENALTY. *Nov. 2, 1999, New York, N.Y. http://www.vatican.va/roman_curia/secretariat_state/documents/rc_seg-st_doc_02111999_death-penalty_en.html*

- Massachusetts Catholic Conference. MASSACHUSETTS CATHOLIC BISHOPS' STATEMENT ON CAPITAL PUNISHMENT. *Feb. 20, 2001. http://www.macathconf.org/dp_statement_feb_2001.htm*

- McCaffrey, Terry. AN INTERVIEW WITH DON CABANA: AN INSIDER'S VIEW OF CAPITAL PUNISHMENT [Video, 60 min.]. *The former warden of Mississippi's Parchman death row unit talks about his moral awakening to the horrors of the death penalty, the friendships he developed with men on death row, and his inability to reconcile his Catholic faith with his role as executioner. Available from Terry McCaffrey, 11154 La Paloma Dr., Cupertino CA 95014.*

- McCarrick, Theodore Cardinal. 101 REASONS TO ABANDON THE DEATH PENALTY. *2000. Statement by chair of U.S. Conference of Catholic Bishops' Domestic Policy Committee on the occasion of the April 2000 release of the 101st person from U.S. death rows since 1973. http://www.usccb.org/sdwp/national/101reasons.htm*

- McCormick, Pat. CATHOLIC WISDOM ON THE DEATH PENALTY. *Chicago: Claretian Publications. 1997. 8 pp. Available from Claretian Publications, 205 W. Monroe St., Chicago IL 60606. Can also be ordered at http://www.uscatholic.org/new.htm#wisdom*

- Megivern, James J. THE DEATH PENALTY: AN HISTORICAL AND THEOLOGICAL SURVEY. *Mahwah, NJ: Paulist Press, 1997. 641 pp. ISBN: 0-8091-0487-3. Theologian traces the development and changes in Catholic Church doctrine on the death penalty throughout the centuries.*

- National Association of State Catholic Conference Directors [Website]. *http://www.nasccd.org. A web page on this site (http://www.nasccd.org/DeathPenalty.htm), contains links to major statements on capital punishment issued by state Catholic Conferences from 1987 to date. Another page on the site (http://www.nasccd.org/StateConferences/Websitetable.htm), has links to the websites of individual state Catholic Conferences, many of which contain statements on the issue and news of current anti-death penalty activities in their respective states.*

- National Jewish-Catholic Consultation. TO END THE DEATH PENALTY: A JOINT STATEMENT OF THE NJCC *(a group co-sponsored by the National Council of Synagogues and the U.S. Conference of Catholic Bishops' Committee on Ecumenical and Interreligious Affairs). 1999. http://www.usccb.org/comm/archives/1999/99-288.htm*

- New Jersey Catholic Conference. CAPITAL PUNISHMENT IN NEW JERSEY: A STATEMENT FROM THE STATE'S CATHOLIC BISHOPS, *Aug. 18, 1999.*

http://www.njcathconf.com/statements/capital_punishment.htm

- New Mexico Catholic Conference. BISHOPS OF NEW MEXICO OPPOSE THE DEATH PENALTY. *Oct. 9, 2001 Statement. www.archdiocesesantafe.org/Offices/Communications/PressReleases/Archived%20Press%20Releases/01.10.09.DeathPen.html*

- New York State Catholic Conference. DEATH IS NOT THE ANSWER: A REAFFIRMATION OF OPPOSITION TO CAPITAL PUNISHMENT BY THE NEW YORK STATE CATHOLIC BISHOPS. *Feb. 15, 1994. http://www.nyscatholicconference.org/statements*

- North Dakota Catholic Conference. REVERENCE FOR LIFE AND THE PRESERVATION OF THE COMMON GOOD: A STATEMENT FROM THE NORTH DAKOTA CATHOLIC CONFERENCE CONCERNING THE DEATH PENALTY. *Jan. 1995. http://ndcatholic.org/DPstmt.htm*

- O'Malley, Sean, O.F.M.Cap. THE GOSPEL OF LIFE VS. THE DEATH PENALTY: PASTORAL LETTER ON CAPITAL PUNISHMENT. *Feb. 25, 1999. http://www.macathconf.org/O'Malley2-25.htm. Pax Christi USA. Statement Regarding the Death Penalty, April 1, 2000. http://www.paxchristiusa.org/news_events_more.asp?id=26*

- Pax Christi USA. BREAKING THE CYCLE OF VIOLENCE. *Packet of materials on the death penalty includes educational information, excerpts from Catholic social teaching, information on the consistent life ethic, a suggested prayer service, and action suggestions. Packet No. 525-410, available from Pax Christi USA, 532 West 8th St., Erie PA 16502. Can also be ordered at http://shop.paxchristiusa.org/shopsite/pax/packets.html*

- Pennsylvania Catholic Conference. THE DEATH PENALTY - CHOOSE LIFE: A STATEMENT ON CAPITAL PUNISHMENT. *Feb. 2001. http://www.pacatholic.org/bishops'%20statements/chooselife.htm*

- Prejean, Helen, C.S.J. DEAD MAN WALKING: AN EYEWITNESS ACCOUNT OF THE DEATH PENALTY IN THE UNITED STATES. *New York: Random House, 1993. 192 pp., ISBN: 0679403582*

(Hardcover). New York: Vintage, 1994. 276 pp., ISBN 0679751319 (Paperback). A Catholic nun recounts her service as spiritual advisor to two death row inmates.

- Prejean, Helen, C.S.J., and Lucille Sarrat. REFLECTIONS ON DEAD MAN WALKING. *Plainfield, NJ: Renew International, 2000. ISBN 0-7648-0564-9. 32 pp. Explores the death penalty in terms of Catholic social teaching and the example of Jesus. Designed for use by both adult and high school reading groups.*

- Ross, Joseph. LIVING AND DYING ON DEATH ROW: AN EYEWITNESS ACCOUNT. *2001. In: 2001-2002 Respect Life Program of the U.S. Conference of Catholic Bishops' Secretariat for Pro-Life Activities. http://www.usccb.org/prolife/programs/rlp/01ros.htm*

- The Roundtable, Association of Diocesan Social Action Directors. CHOOSE LIFE: BUILDING OPPOSITION TO THE DEATH PENALTY. *New York: National Pastoral Life Center. 2000. 32 pp. Practical tips in the areas of conversion, public awareness, and public advocacy. Available from NPLC, 18 Bleecker St., New York, NY 10012. Can also be ordered at http://www.nplc.org/pub/roundtable.asp*

- Texas Catholic Conference. STATEMENT BY THE CATHOLIC BISHOPS OF TEXAS ON CAPITAL PUNISHMENT. *Oct. 1997. Statement by the Catholic Bishops of Texas Opposing the Execution of the Mentally Retarded, 1998. http://www.txcatholic.org/Public_Policy.htm*

- United States Conference of Catholic Bishops: DIOCESAN DIRECTORY [Website]. *http://www.usccb.org/dioceses.htm. Site has links to the website addresses of all U.S. archdiocese and dioceses, many of which contain statements and news about anti-death penalty activities on the diocesan level.*

- United States Conference of Catholic Bishops: DEPARTMENT OF SOCIAL DEVELOPMENT AND WORLD PEACE [Website]. *http://www.usccb.org/sdwp/national/dea.htm. Site contains links to major statements by the U.S. bishops' national conference as well as those of state conferences and individual dioceses.*

- United States Conference of Catholic Bishops: SECRETARIAT FOR PRO-LIFE ACTIVITIES [Website]. *http://www.usccb.org/prolife/issues/cappunish/index.htm. Site contains articles from the Secretariat's bimonthly Life Issues newsletter and its annual* Respect *Life Program packet for parishes.*
- United States Conference of Catholic Bishops. STATEMENT ON CAPITAL PUNISHMENT. *1980. 21 pp. Publication 740-5, available from USCCB, 3211 4th St. N.E., Washington, DC 20017. Can also be downloaded from http://www.usccb.org/sdwp/national/criminal/death/uscc80.htm*
- United States Conference of Catholic Bishops. CONFRONTING A CULTURE OF VIOLENCE: A PASTORAL MESSAGE OF THE U.S. CATHOLIC BISHOPS. *1994. 36 pp. (English); 40 pp. (Spanish). Publication 028-1 (English) and 045-1 (Spanish), available from USCCB, 3211 4th St. N.E., Washington, DC 20017. Can also be downloaded from http://www.usccb.org/sdwp/national/criminal/ccv94.htm*
- United States Conference of Catholic Bishops. A GOOD FRIDAY APPEAL TO END THE DEATH PENALTY. *Washington, DC: USCCB. 1999. 6 pp. ISBN 1-57455-327-5. A March, 1999 statement of the conference's Administrative Board. Publication 5-327 (English) and 5-821 (Spanish), available from USCCB, 3211 4th St. N.E., Washington, DC 20017. Can also be downloaded from http://www.usccb.org/sdwp/national/criminal/appeal.htm*
- United States Conference of Catholic Bishops. RESPONSIBILITY, REHABILITATION, AND RESTORATION: A CATHOLIC PERSPECTIVE ON CRIME AND CRIMINAL JUSTICE. *2000. 64 pp. (English); 82 pp. (Spanish). Text of a Nov. 15, 2000 statement by the U.S. bishops; includes a renewed call for an end to the death penalty. Publication 5-394 (English) and 5-846 (Spanish). Available from USCCB,*

- *3211 4th St. N.E., Washington, DC 20017. Can also be downloaded from http://www.usccb.org/sdwp/criminal.htm*
- Wisconsin Catholic Conference. CAPITAL PUNISHMENT IN WISCONSIN: A STATEMENT FROM THE STATE'S ROMAN CATHOLIC BISHOPS. *June 1995. http://www.wisconsincatholic.org/statements/punishment.html*

APPENDIX 2

EXTENDED BIBLIOGRAPHY ON RESTORATIVE JUSTICE

MARK WOLFF, J.D., LL.M.
Professor of Law
Saint Thomas University School of Law
Miami Gardens, Florida

- American Bar Association. 1990. *Dispute Resolution Program Directory 1990.* Washington, DC: American Bar Association Standing Committee on Dispute Resolution.
- Anderson, K. 1982. "Community justice centers – alternatives to prosecution." In P. Grabosky (ed.). *National Symposium on Victimology - Proceedings.* Phillip Act, Australia: Australian Institute of Criminology, p. 57-74.
- Aubuchon, J. 1978. "Model for community diversion." *Canadian Journal of Criminology.* 20(3): 296-300.
- Baines, C., P. Evans and S. Neysmith (eds.). 1991. *Women's Caring: Feminist Perspectives on Social Welfare.* Toronto ON: McClelland & Stewart.
- Barnes, B. and P. Adler. 1983. "Meditation and lawyers - the Pacific way-a view from Hawaii." *Hawaii Bar Journal.* 18(1): 37-51.

- Barnett, R. 1977. "Restitution: A new paradigm of criminal justice." *Ethics: An International Journal of Social, Political and Legal Philosophy.* 87(4):279-301
- Bazemore, G. and L. Walgrave. 1999. "Restorative juvenile justice: In search of fundamentals and an outline for systemic reform." In G. Bazemore and L. Walgrave (eds.) *Restorative Juvenile Justice: Repairing the Harm of Youth Crime.* Monsey, NY: Criminal Justice Press.
- Bazemore. G. *1993 Balanced and Restorative Justice for Juvenile Offenders: An Overview of a New OJJDP Initiative.* Washington DC: Office of Juvenile Justice and Delinquency Prevention.
- Bonafé-Schmitt, J-P. 1992. "Penal and community mediation: The case of France." In H. Messmer & H.-U. Otto (eds.). *Restorative Justice on Trial. Pitfalls and Potentials of Victim-Offender Mediation-International Research Perspectives.* Netherlands: Kluwer, p. 179-196.
- Bowen, Helen and Consedine, Jim (eds.)1998, Restorative *Justice Contemporary Themes and Practices.* Ploughshares Publications, Christchurch, New Zealand.
- Boyack, Jim 1998. "How Sayest the Court of Appeal" in Bowen Helen & Consedine, Jim (eds), *Restorative Justice Contemporary Themes and Practices.*
- Braithwaite, J. 1996. "Restorative justice and a better future." Dorothy J. Killam Memorial Lecture. Dalhousie University, October.
- Braithwaite, J. 1997. "Restorative justice is republican justice." Paper presented at Restorative Justice for Juveniles. Potentialities, Risks and Problems for Research, Leuven, Belgium, May 12-14.

- Braithwaite, J. 1999. "Democracy, Community and Problem Solving." Paper presented at Building Strong Partnerships for Restorative Practice. Burlington VT, Aug. 5-7.
- Braithwaite, J. and S. Mugford. 1994. "Conditions of successful reintegration ceremonies." *British Journal Of Criminology*. 34(2): 139-71.
- Braithwaite, John. 1989. Crimes, Shame and Reintegration. Cambridge: Cambridge University Press, 1989.
- Braithwaite, John and Philip Pettit 1990. *Not Just Deserts: A Republican Theory of Criminal Justice.* Oxford: Oxford University Press.
- Burford, G. and J. Pennell. 1994a. "A Canadian innovation of family group decision making." In *International Year of the Family Conference: Strengthening Families.* Wellington, NZ: New Zealand Social Welfare Department, p. 40-49.
- Burford, G. and J. Pennell. 1994b. "New roles for old partners in resolving family Violence." In Proceedings of Beyond Badgley: *Responses to the Report Sexual Offences Against Children.* National Clearinghouse on Family Violence, Health Programs and Services Branch. Ottawa, ON: Health Canada, p. 45-47.
- Burford G. and J. Pennell. 1995a. *Family Group Decision Making Project: Implementation Report Summary.* St. John's, NewFoundland, CAN: Family Group Decision Making Project, School of Social Work, Memorial University of Newfoundland.
- Burford, G. and J. Pennell. 1995b. "Family group decision making: An innovation in child and family welfare." In J. Hudson and B. Galaway (Eds.). *Child Welfare in Canada: Research and Policy Implications.* Toronto, ON: Thompson Educational Publishing.

- Burford, G. and J. Pennell. 1996. "Family group decision making: generating Indigenous structures for resolving family violence." *Protecting Children.* 12(3): 17-21.
- Burford, G. and J. Pennell. 1997. Family Group Decision Making. *Outcome Report Summary. Memorial University of Newfoundland, School of Social Work.* Bush, R. and J. Folger. 1994. The Promise of Mediation. San Francisco: Jossey-Bass.
- Bushie, J. 1997. "CHCH Reflections." In *Ministry of the Solicitor General of Canada. The Four Circles of Hollow Water. Aboriginal Peoples Collection.* Cat. No.: JS5-1/15-1997E. Ottawa, Canada: Public Works and Government Services. http://www.sgc.gc.ca/epub/abocor/e199703/e199703.htm.
- Cameron, L. and M. Thorsborne. 1999. "Restorative justice and school discipline: Mutually exclusive?" Paper presented at the Restorative Justice and Civil Society. Australian National University, Canberra, February 16-18.
- Christie, N. 1977. "Conflict as property." *British Journal of Criminology* 17(1): 1-14. Claassen, R. 1995. "Restorative justice principles and evaluation continuums." Paper presented at National Center for Peacemaking and Conflict Resolution, Fresno Pacific College, May.
- Community Justice Initiatives Association. 1983. *Mediation Primer: A Training Guide for Mediators in the Criminal Justice System.* Kitchener, On.: Community Justice Initiatives of Waterloo Region.
- Connolly, M. and M. McKenzie. 1999. Effective Participatory Practice. Family Group Conferencing in Child Protection. New York: Aldine de Gruyter.
- Consedine, J. 1995. *Restorative Justice: Healing the Effects of Crime.* New Zealand: Ploughshares Publications.

- Consedine, J. and H. Bowen. 1999. *Restorative Justice – Contemporary Themes and Practice.* New Zealand: Ploughshares Publications.
- Consedine, Jim. *Restorative Justice: Healing the Effects of Crime.* Lyttleton, New Zealand: Ploughshares Publications, 1995.
- Cordella, J. 1991. "Reconciliation and the mutualist model of community." In H. Pepinsky & R. Quinney (eds.). *Criminology as Peacemaking.* Bloomington: Indiana University Press, pp. 30-46.
- Cragg, W. 1992 *The Practice of Punishment: Towards a Theory of Restorative Justice.* London: Routiedge.
- Cutshall, C. and P. McCold. 1983. "Patterns of Stock Theft Victimization and Formal Response Strategies Among the Ila of Zambia." *Victimology* 7(1-4): 137-155.
- Dickson-Gilmore, E. 1992. "Finding the ways of the ancestors: Cultural change and the invention of tradition in the development of separate legal systems." *Canadian Journal of Criminology,* 34(3-4): 479-502.
- Dignan, J. 1992. "Repairing the Damage: Can Reparation Work in the Service of Diversion?" *British Journal of Criminology* 32: 453-72.
- Evarts, W. 1990. "Compensation through mediation: a conceptual framework." In B. Galaway and J. Hudson (eds.). *Criminal Justice, Restitution and Reconciliation.* Monsey NY: Criminal Justice Press, pp. 15-21.
- Falck, S. 1992. "The Norwegian community mediation centers at a crossroads." In H. Messmer and H.-U. Otto (eds.). *Restorative Justice on Trial. Pitfalls and Potentials of Victim-Offender Mediation-International Research Perspectives.* Netherlands: Kluwer Academic Publishers, pp. 131-148.

- Filner, J., M. Ostermeyer, and C. Bethel. 1995. *Compendium of State Court Resource Materials*, Washington, DC: National Institute for Dispute Resolution.
- Fogel, D., B. Galaway and J. Hudson. 1972. "Restitution in criminal justice: A Minnesota experiment." *Criminal Law Bulletin.* 8(8): 681-691.
- Galaway, B. 1977. "Restitution as an integrative punishment." In R. Barnett and J. Hagel (eds.). *Assessing the Criminal: Restitution, Retribution and the Legal Process.* Cambridge, MA: Ballinger, pp. 331-347.
- Galaway, B. 1988. "Restitution as innovation or unfilled promise?" *Federal Probation* 52 (3): 3-14.
- Galaway, B. 1992. "The New Zealand experience implementing the reparation sentence." In H.Messmer and H.-U. Otto (eds.). *Restorative justice on Trial. Pitfalls and Potentials of Victim-Offender Mediation-International Research Perspectives.* Netherlands: Kluwer Academic Publishers, pp. 55-80.
- Galaway, B. 1995. "Victim-offender mediation by New Zealand probation officers: the possibilities and the reality." *Mediation Quarterly.* 12(3): 249-262.
- Goldstein, H. 1990. *Problem-Oriented Policing.* Philadelphia, Pa.: Temple University Press.
- Graber, L., T. Keys and J. White. 1996. "Family group decision-making in the United States: The case of Oregon." In J. Hudson, et al. (eds.). *Family Group Conferences: Perspectives on Policy and Practice.* Monsey, NY: Criminal Justice Press, pp. 180-194.
- Graham, I. 1993. "Juvenile Justice in New South Wales." In L. Atkinson and S-A. Gerull (eds.). *New Directions In National Conference on Juvenile Justice Conference Proceedings No. 22*, Canberra, Australia: Australian institute of Criminology, pp. 149-166.

- Hardin, M. 1996. *Family Group Conferences in Child Abuse and Neglect Cases: Learning from the Expereince of New Zealand.* Washington DC: ABA Center on Children and the Law.
- Hassall, I. 1996. "Origin and development of family group conferences." In J. Hudson, et al. (eds.). *Family Group Conferences: Perspectives on Policy and Practice.* Monsey, NY: Criminal Justice Press, pp. 17-36.
- Hudson, J. and B. Galaway. 1974. "Undoing the wrong." *Social Work.* 19(3): 313-318.
- Hyndman, M., D.B. Moore and M. Thorsborne. 1995. "Family and community conferences in schools." In R. Homel (ed.). *Preventive Criminology.* Brisbane, AUS: Griffith University.
- Jackson, Moana. 1998. *The Maori in the Criminal Justice System: He Waipaanga Hou - A New Perspective.* Department of Justice, Wellington.
- Korn, R. 1971. "Of crime, criminal justice and corrections." *University of San Francisco Law Review.* 6(1): 27-75.
- Laster, R E. 1970. "Criminal restitution: a survey of its past history and an analysis of its present usefulness." *University of Richmond Law Review* 5(1):71-98.
- Marsh, P. and G. Crow. 1998. Family Group Conferences in Child Welfare. Oxford: Blackwell Sciences Ltd.
- Marshal T. F. (1997). "Seeking the Whole Justice," paper to ISTD Conference Bristol University.
- Marshall, T. 1992. "Restorative Justice on Trial in Britain." In H. Messmer and H.-U. Otto (eds.). *Restorative Justice on Trial. Pitfalls and Potentials of Victim-Offender Mediation-International Research Perspectives.* Netherlands: Kluwer Academic Publishers, pp. 15-28.

- Maxwell, G. 1996. "A Restorative Justice: A Maori Perspective." The New Zealand Maori Council. Wellingtin, NZ: Ministry of Justice.
- Maxwell, Gabrielle. 1998*Restorative Process and Outcome: Emerging Theories of Restorative Justice – Changing Hearts and Minds*, Wellington, November.
- McCold, P. 1996. "Restorative Justice and the Role of Community." In B. Galaway and J. Hudson (eds.) *Restorative Justice: International Perspectives.* Monsesy, NY: Criminal Justice Press.
- McCold, P. and B. Wachtel. 1998a. "Community is Not a Place: A New Look at Community Justice Initiatives." *Contemporary Justice Review.*1 (1): 71-85, 1998
- McCold, P. and B. Wachtel. 1998b. *Restorative Policing Experiment: The Bethlehem Pennsylvania Police Family Group Conferencing Project.* U.S. Dept. of Justice, National Institute of Justice. Washington DC: U.S. Govt. Printing Office.
- McDonald, J. and D.B. Moore. 1999. "Community conferencing as a special case of conflict transformation. Paper presented to Restorative Justice and Civil Society. Australian National University, Canberra, February 16-18.
- McElrea, F.W.M. (ed) 1995. *Re-thinking Criminal Justice* Vol 1 *Justice in the Community*, Victoria University, Wellington, New Zealand.
- McElrea, F.W.M.,1994. "Restorative Justice. The New Zealand Youth Court: A Model for Development in Other Courts" in *Public Sector* 17(3).
- Merry, S. and N. Milner (eds.). 1995. *The Possibility of Popular Justice. A case study of community mediation in the United States.* Ann Arbor, MI: University of Michigan Press.

- Ministry of Justice New Zealand, (1998). *Restorative Justice The Public Submissions*, Wellington, New Zealand, 17.
- Moore, D B. 1993. Shame, forgiveness, and juvenile justice. *Criminal justice Ethics* 12(1), 3-25.
- New Zealand Maori Council.1998. "Restorative Justice: A Mori Perspective" in Bowen, Helen and Consedine Jim (eds), *Restorative Justice Contemporary Theses and Practices.*
- Nicholl, C. 1998. *Implementing Restorative Justice. A toolbox for the implementation of restorative justice and the advancement of community policing.* Office of Community Oriented Policing Services. U.S. Department of Justice, Washington DC.
- Olsen, T., G. Maxwell and A. Morris. 1995. "Maori and youth justice in New Zealand." In K. Hazlehurst (ed.). *Popular Justice and Community Regeneration.* London, UK: Praeger, pp. 89-102
- Peachey, D. 1989. 'The Kitchener experiment." In M. Wright and B. Galaway (eds.). *Mediation and Criminal Justice. Victims, Offenders and Community.* London: Sage.
- Pennel, J. and G. Burford. 1994. "Widening the circle: Family group decision making." *Journal of Child and Youth Care.* (1): 1-11.
- Pepinsky, H. E. and R. Quinney (eds.).1991. *Criminology as Peacemaking.* Bloomington: Indiana University Press.
- Perry, L., T. Lajeunesse & A. Woods. 1987. *Mediation Services: An Evaluation.* Manitoba, Canada: Manitoba Attorney General.
- Peters, Tony and Ivo Aertsen, "Restorative Justice: In Search of New Avenues in the Judicial Dealing with Crime: The Presentation of a Project of Mediation for Reparation:," in C. Fijnaut et. al. (ed.) *Changes in Society, Crime and Criminal Justice in Europe.* Antwerpen: Kluwer Law and Taxation Publishers, 1995.

- Pettit, Philip with John Braithwaite, 1993. "Not Just Deserts Even in Sentencing," *Current Issues in Criminal Justice* 4:225-35, 1993.

- Pranis, K. 1997. "Restoring community: The process of circle sentencing." Paper presented at Justice Without Violence: Views from Peacemaking Criminology and Restorative Justice, Albany, New York, June 6.

- Pratt, J. 1996. "Colonization, power and silence: A history of indigenous justice in New Zealand society." In B. Galaway and J. Hudson (eds.). *Restorative Justice: International Perspective.* Monesy, NY: Criminal Justice Press, pp. 137-156.

- Retzinger, S. and T. Scheff. 1996. "Strategy for community conferences: Emotions and social bonds." In B. Galaway and J. Hudson (eds.). *Restorative Justice: International Perspective.* Monesy, NY: Criminal Justice Press, pp. 315-336.

- Ross, R. 1994. "Dueling Paradigms? Western criminal justice versus Aboriginal community healing." In R. Gosse, J. Y. Henderson & R. Carter (eds.), *Continuing Poundmaker & Riel's Quest* (pp. 241-268). Saskatoon: Purich.

- Rowe, K. 1985. "Limits of the neighborhood justice center: Why domestic violence cases should not be mediated." *Emory Law Journal.* 34(3-4): 855-910.

- Ruth-Heffelbower, D. 1996. "Toward a Christian Theology of Church and Society as it Relates to Restorative Justice." Presentation to 4th Annual Restorative Justice Conference, Fresno, CA, October 25.

- Sherman, L., H. Strand, G. Barnes, J. Braithwaite, N. Inkpen and M.M. Teh. 1998. *Experiments in Restorative Policing. A Progress Report on the Canberra Reintegrative Shaming Experiments (RISE) to the*

- *National Police Research Unit.* Canberra ACT: Australian National University. http://www.aic.gov.au/rjustice/progress/index.html
- Sobey, B. 1998. "Conferencing in Australia. A Discussion Paper." Diversionary Conferencing Advisory Committee, Australian Federal Police, June.
- Spier, P. 1995. *Conviction and Sentencing of Offenders in NZ; 1985-1994.* Department of Justice, Wellington, New Zealand.
- Stuart, B. 1996. "Circle sentencing: Turning swords into ploughshares." In B. Galaway and J. Hudson (eds.). *Restorative Justice: International Perspectives.* Monsey, NY: Criminal Justice Press, pp. 193-206.
- Taraschi, S. 1998. "Peacemaking criminology and aboriginal justice initiatives as a revitalization of justice." *Contemporary Justice Review.* 1(1): 103-121.
- United States Department of Justice, Bureau of Justice Statistics. http://www.ojp.usdoj.gov/gjs/welcome.html
- Van Ness, D. and K. Heetderks. 1197. *Restoring Justice.* Cincinnati, OH: Anderson Publishing Company.
- Victim Offender Reconciliation Resource Center. 1984. *The VORP Book. An Organizational and Operation Manual.* Valpariso, IN: PACT Institute of Justice.
- Wachtel, T. 1998. *Real Justice.* Pipersville PA: Piper's Press.
- Walgrave, L. 1995."Restorative Justice for Juveniles: Just a Technique or a Fully Fledged Alternative?" *The Howard Journal* 34(3): 228-249.
- Walgrave, L. 1999. "Community service as a cornerstone of systemic restorative response to juvenile justice." In G. Bazemore & L. Walgrave (eds.). *Restorative Juvenile Justice: Repairing the Harm of Youth Crime.* Monsey NY: Criminal Justice Press.

- Ward, A. 1995. *A show of Justice: Racial 'Amalgamation' in 19th Century New Zealand*, 2nd ed, Auckland University Press, Auckland, New Zealand.
- Warner, S. 1992. "Reparation, mediation and Scottish criminal justice." In H. Messmer & H.-U. Otto (eds.) *Restorative Justice Trial: Pitfalls and Potentials of Victim-Offender Mediation-International Research Perspectives*. Netherlands: Kluwer Academic.
- Wundersitz, J. and S. Hetzel. 1996. "Family Conferencing for Young Offenders: the South Australian Experience." In J. Hudson, et al. (eds.) *Family Group Conferences: Perspectives on Policy and Practice*. Monsey, NY: Criminal Justice Press.
- Yazzie, R. 1994. "Life comes form it: Navajo justice concepts." *New Mexico Law Review*. 24:175-190.
- Yazzie, R. 1998. "Navajo peacemaking: Implications for adjudication-based systems of justice." *Contemporary Justice Review*. 1(1): 123-131.
- Yazzie, R., and J. Zion. 1996. "Navajo restorative justice: The law of equity and harmony." In B. Galaway and J. Hudson (eds.). *Restorative Justice: International Perspectives*. Monsey, NY: Criminal Justice Press.
- Young, M A. 1995. "Restorative Community Justice: A Call to Action." Washington, DC: National Organization for Victim Assistance.
- Zehr, Howard. "Rethinking Criminal Justice: Restorative Justice" in McElrea FWM (ed.), *Re-thinking Criminal Justice Vol 1, Justice in the Community*.
- Zehr, Howard. 1980. "Mediating the victim-offender conflict." *New Perspectives on Crime and Justice* (Issue #2). Mennonite Central Committee Office of Criminal Justice, Akron, PA.

- Zehr, Howard. 1985. "Retributive Justice, Restorative Justice." *New Perspectives on Crime and Justice* (Issue #4). Mennonite Central Committee Office of Criminal Justice, Akron, PA.
- Zehr, Howard. 1990. *Changing Lenses: A New Focus for Crime and Justice.* Scottsdale, PA: Herald Press.
- Zehr, Howard and H. Mika. 1998. "Fundamental concepts of restorative justice." *Contemporary Justice Review.* 1(1): 41-55.

FLORIDA COUNCIL OF CATHOLIC SCHOLARSHIP

"Wisdom is a tree of life"
Proverbs 3:18

The Florida Council of Catholic Scholarship
is a scholarly society established in December 1996
at the invitation of the Florida Catholic Conference.
It is hosted by Saint Thomas University
of Miami Gardens, Florida

The mission of the Council is
to serve the Catholic churches of Florida
in undertaking a new evangelization in response to
the great ecological, social, and spiritual crises of late modern society.
This is to be done by means of interdisciplinary studies
fostering a fresh dialogue between faith and culture
in the light of Catholic social teaching.
This dialogue is open to scholars of all faith traditions.

The Council is sponsored by
Barry University,
Blessed Edmund Rice School for Pastoral Ministry,
Saint John Vianney College Seminary,
Saint Leo University,
Saint Thomas University,
Saint Vincent de Paul Regional Seminary.

CATHOLIC MOVEMENT FOR
INTELLECTUAL & CULTURAL AFFAIRS USA

Networking Catholic Intellectuals, Professionals, and University Students in support of Catholic Social Teaching for the New Globalization

Present on five continents and in 80 countries, the global Pax Romana movement is an international network of 420,000 lay Catholic intellectuals, professionals, and students devoted to the study, application, and advancement of Catholic social teaching about human dignity, family, work, human rights, justice, peace, and ecology in local, national, and global society. Its present membership base is now growing rapidly in Africa, Asia, and Latin America.

The roots of the movement go back to visionary European Catholic lay leaders who helped Pope Leo XIII to create his 1891 landmark social encyclical, *Rerum Novarum*. The movement began in 1887, became a formal international structure in 1921, and was represented at the League of Nations.

In a meeting with leaders of the movement, Pope Benedict XV gave it the name of "my Pax Romana" – referring to the spirit of peace and reconciliation that its members were fostering after World War I. Later Pope Paul VI, before becoming pope, served as the Pax Romana chaplain for Italy, and Pope John Paul II, also before becoming pope, served as the Pax Romana chaplain for Poland.

In 1947 the movement reorganized into two branches: 1) the International Catholic Movement for Intellectual and Cultural Affairs (ICMICA-MIIC) for professionals and intellectuals; and 2) the International Movement of Catholic Students (IMCS-MIEC) for university students – with both constituting Pax Romana. In the United States the Pax Romana organizations are: 1) Pax Romana/Catholic Movement for Intellectual and Cultural Affairs - USA (PR/CMICA-USA); and 2) the National Coalition of Catholic Students (NCSC).

The global Pax Romana movement is an official non-governmental organization (NGO) accredited to the United Nations, where it holds the highest level consultative status with the UN's Economic and Social Council. It maintains NGO missions at UN centers in New York, Geneva, Vienna, and Paris. In Barcelona the movement has a legal research and action center for international human rights. In Geneva it has a human-rights training program in which interns work with the UN Human Rights office there. In Florida it sponsors the Pax Romana Center for International Study of Catholic Social Teaching and the Global Leadership Program, both at St. Thomas University in Miami Gardens. In New York City, it co-sponsors with St. Thomas University School of Law a semester-long internship program at the United Nations, in which law students become Pax Romana NGO representatives to the UN. Pax Romana is also an official International Catholic Organization (ICO) accredited to the Holy See, and officially participates in the shaping of Catholic social teaching. In addition, Pax Romana hosts specialized international secretariats for artists, teachers, engineers, agronomists, business people, jurists, and scientists.

For more information about Pax Romana, consult the website of the Pax Romana Center for International Study of Catholic Social Teaching at www.pax-romana-center-cst.org, or send an email to paxromana@stu.edu.

PAX ROMANA/CMICA-USA *is a non-profit tax-exempt Catholic lay organization incorporated in Washington DC and listed in the Official Catholic Directory under the Archdiocese of Washington. Contributions to it are welcome and are tax-exempt. The Pension Protection Act of 2006 allows taxpayer-donors to direct charitable transfers from their Individual Retirement Accounts (IRA). If the donor or couple is 70.5 years of age or older, he or she may be eligible to transfer up to $100,000 each or $200,000 per couple to charity from their IRA in 2006 and 2007. Please consult your legal and financial adviser.*

CATHOLIC MOVEMENT FOR
INTELLECTUAL & CULTURAL AFFAIRS USA

Networking Catholic Intellectuals, Professionals, and University Students in support of Catholic Social Teaching

Name(s) ____

Address Line 1 ____

Address Line 2 ____

City State Postal Code ____________________________________

Country ____________________ Date ____________________

Phone ____________________ Email ____________________

Profession(s) ____

Membership Application: *(Please include brief bio or resume with this application)*

☐	Individual Membership	$25	☐	Visionary Membership	$250
☐	Family Membership	$35	☐	Patron Membership	$500
☐	Supporting Membership	$50	☐	Angel Membership	$1000
☐	Sustaining Membership	$100	☐	Student Associate	*Free*

Donor Contribution:

☐	Contributing Friend	$25	☐	Visionary Friend	$250
☐	Supporting Friend	$50	☐	Patron Friend	$500
☐	Sustaining Friend	$100	☐	Angel Friend	$1000

Fill out this page, tear it out of the book, and mail it to the address below.
Make your check payable to PAX ROMANA CMICA-USA

PAX ROMANA
Catholic Movement for Intellectual and Cultural Affairs
USA
PO Box 65302, Washington, DC 20035 USA
Phone +1 (202) 269.6672 / Email: membership@pax-romana-cmica-usa.org
Website: www.pax-romana-cmica-usa.org

THANK YOU FOR SUPPORTING CATHOLIC SOCIAL TEACHING!

ORDER FORM FOR BOOK:
BEYOND THE DEATH PENALTY

Tear this page out of the book and fill it out.

Name(s) ____

Address Line 1 ______________________________________

Address Line 2 ______________________________________

City State Postal Code _________________________________

Country ____________________ Date ___________________________

Phone ____________________ Email ___________________________

1	Price of Book:	**$13.99**
2	List number of copies requested:	
3	Calculate subtotal (*multiply price by number of copies*):	
4	Calculate member-friend discount (*multiply subtotal by 20%*):	
5	Discounted cost (*subtract discount from subtotal*)	
6	Shipping/Handling (*multiply number of copies by $4.00*):	
7	TOTAL (*add amount on line 3 or 5 to amount on line 6*):	

Discount above is for dues-paying Members or contributing Friends of Pax Romana.
For orders of more than 5 copies or for international orders, call for special pricing.
Please make your check payable to PAX ROMANA CMICA-USA
Mail this sheet and your check to the address below.

PAX ROMANA CENTER
FOR INTERNATIONAL STUDY OF CATHOLIC SOCIAL TEACHING
Saint Thomas University, 16401 NW 37th Avenue, Miami Gardens, Florida 33054 USA
Phone +1 (305) 474.6913 / Fax +1 (305) 474.6915 / Email: paxromana@stu.edu
Website: www.pax-romana-center-cst.org

THANK YOU FOR SUPPORTING CATHOLIC SOCIAL TEACHING!

www.ingramcontent.com/pod-product-compliance
Lightning Source LLC
Chambersburg PA
CBHW030313290526
45785CB00001B/332

9781419673108